COLORADO HOT SPRINGS GUIDE

COLORADO HOT SPRINGS GUIDE

Second Edition,
Revised and Updated

RICK CAHILL

PRUETT PUBLISHING COMPANY
BOULDER, COLORADO

 Address all inquiries to: Pruett Publishing Company, 2928 Pearl Street, Boulder, Colorado 80301.

Printed in the United States
10 9 8 7 6 5 4 3 2 1

Library of Congress Cataloging-in-Publication Data

Cahill, Rick, 1950-
Colorado Hot Springs guide / Rick Cahill. — 2nd ed. rev. and updated.
p. cm.
Includes bibliographical references and index.
ISBN 0-87108-843-6
1. Hot springs—Colorado. I. Title.
GB1198.3.C6C33 1994
917.880433—dc20 94-682
CIP

Cover and book design by Jody Chapel, Cover to Cover Design

For the people of Colorado

Contents

Acknowledgments

I owe special thanks to the editor of the first edition of *Colorado Hot Springs Guide,* Gerald Keenan, for introducing me to the world of book publishing. I also wish to thank all the resort owners for being so gracious; Carrie Carson for helping with everything; Wilma Burke of the Eldorado Springs Historical Society for photos and good conversation; Richard H. Pearl of the Colorado Geological Survey for checking the geological accuracy of the manuscript and also for providing me with *Bulletin 39,* a most valuable tool for locating the springs; Kevin McCarthy, who generously shared his knowledge of a subject on which he has done considerable research; the librarians in the Western Historical Collections of the University of Colorado for digging up dusty documents and old photos; Lyn Reed and Lynn Clarke of the Boulder Public Library for being so helpful; Ron Dwinell for helping a stranded motorist; my brother Tim for advice; Rich for driving and having the sense not to drive me crazy; and Willie Nelson for writing the song "On the Road Again." I am also especially indebted to Randy Gates for using his always awesome computer skills to update the maps and graphics in the second edition.

Author's Note

These reports and reflections on Colorado's hot springs are drawn from months of travel and research. For the most part, I wrote each section of the book immediately after visiting an area in order to give the reader the most accurate and authentic picture of each hot spring.

Some springs are located on private property, and strict rules of conduct are imposed on visitors there. Other springs are located in the wilderness, where rules are less defined. There are no laws against skinny-dipping in remote wilderness areas if those present are consenting adults; however, if the "intent to offend" can be proven legally, skinny-dipping constitutes a crime of indecent exposure. This is something to keep in mind when wilderness areas are crowded with hikers.

One very important caution: People with high blood pressure and heart trouble are advised to check with their physicians before using hot springs. And alcohol and other drugs should be used in moderation, if at all, around hot springs, because high altitudes combined with the high temperature of the water will make the effects of such substances much more volatile and unpredictable.

Each spring has its own unique character. Readers are advised to read each description carefully to prevent inconvenience or embarrassment. Keep in mind that attitudes toward hot-springing change rapidly. If in doubt, check with local authorities.

Introduction

Colorado is a good state, and a great state as far as recreation goes. It has the best of everything. But there is one form of recreation that has been overlooked in the last few decades, a form of recreation that both older and younger generations can enjoy: hot springs!

Not long ago, the sophisticated traveler was likely to sneer at hot-spring health spas. Visions of smelly watering holes for little old ladies with tired blood and feet blurred the picture. But all that has changed with the swiftness of fashion.

Colorado's hot springs are legendary—they're fun in the summer as well as the winter. Not only that, but they're inexpensive, and some are even free. Hot springs come in a variety of shapes and sizes. There are hot-spring health spas and historic hot-spring resorts that will give you a sense of life as it must have been lived in a gracious and perhaps more romantic time. There are hot springs located near ski slopes, and there are hot springs that even the dedicated hiker and cross-country skier will find a challenge to reach. Hot springs are for everybody, and out of the fifty-eight thermal areas located in Colorado's majestic high country, you're sure to find one that is tailor-made for you.

Health nuts are in for a real organic treat. Hot springs are full of life-giving minerals from holy Mother Earth—minerals that are absorbed into the human body through the skin and lungs. Some doctors prescribe the use of hot springs in the treating of obesity because soaking in hot mineral water is a very efficient way of drawing excess water out of the system. Muscular pains and rheumatism have also been improved by soaking in hot springs, and many people suffering from acute anxiety attacks find a soothing soak to be the best sedative on the market. Some, like Cleopatra and Ponce de Leon, have even claimed that mineral springs turn back the aging clock.

There are, in round numbers, about 12 million tourists visiting Colorado each year, and very few of them are aware of this unique form of recreation. This guide is not only designed to help you locate hot springs easily and quickly, but also to help you choose the hot springs that are really right for you. The state map will show you in what counties the springs are located. You can then look up the springs in the table of contents for more specific directions, a composite map, and a general description. At the beginning of each section there is a list of vital information. The geological data; specifically, the flow and temperature, is taken directly from the spring and not the pool. The book also includes a bit of history and a few anecdotes to add local color. If some of the stories seem like fables, it is because Colorado and its people are fabulous. Who knows why this part of the country produced so many mighty individuals? Perhaps there is something in the water.

If you're a cross-country motorist entertaining a terrible backache, a health seeker, a serious gourmet bather, or just someone who is interested in the history or geography of Colorado, this book is for you. Don't wait another minute! Stake your claim to Colorado's best, and enjoy hot-spring time in the Rockies year-round.

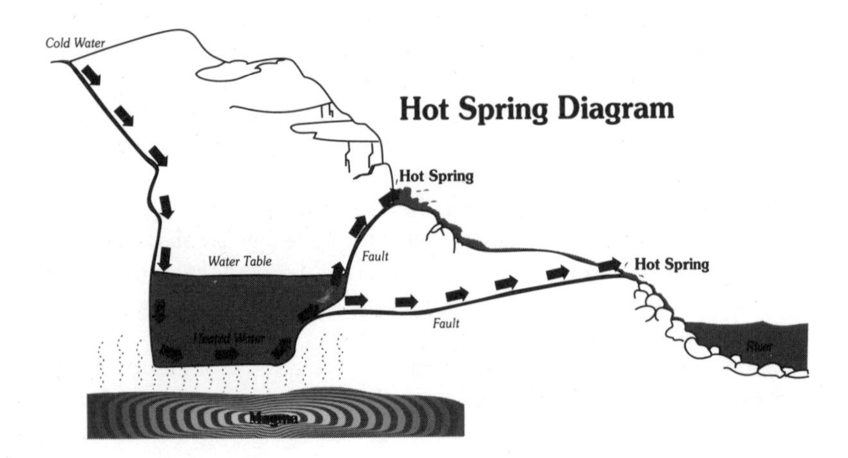

A Bit of History

In the beginning were the mighty Rockies. Nearby were many bubbling mineral springs where great prehistoric beasts came to drink. Then there were the bears, Indians, Spaniards, and fur trappers who made their homes here. And now there are highways, treeless suburbs, and endless chains of fast-food restaurants that snake around the forgotten fountains.

A little more than a century ago, only dusty Indian trails led to Colorado's many hot springs. The Indians considered springs sacred places, for they believed that the Great Spirit lived there deep in the bowels of the earth. Each year when the snows melted, various tribes came to these consecrated waters and set up tepees covered with red elk skins. Bathing rituals took place that supposedly brought good luck when the Indians moved on to their summer hunting grounds. These springs were also used as sacrificial altars. Before going into battle, the Indians often left gifts of animal skins, eagle feathers, and scalps to encourage their god to bring them victory. After the fighting, they returned to the Big Medicine fountains with their sick and wounded, seeking new strength and vitality.

Although most of Colorado's hot springs were considered neutral sanctuaries by the Indians, the possession of Pagosa Springs was long disputed by the Utes and the Navajos. In 1866 the struggle came to an end when the warring Indians arranged a duel between the best warrior of each tribe. The Utes picked a United States Army officer, Colonel Albert H. Pfeiffer, who had fought many Indian battles and was respected so much that he had been adopted into the tribe. The Navajos chose their strongest warrior, a giant with a fierce reputation as a bloodthirsty killer. Each man was to go into combat naked and armed only with a Bowie knife. These were the conditions set by the leaders of each tribe. Pfeiffer was a thin, wiry man, and although his chances of survival looked meager against his massive opponent, he proved to be a good choice for the Utes. When the duel began, he hurled his Bowie knife deep into the Navajo warrior's chest. The brave dropped to his knees and died in a pool of blood. The Utes immediately took possession of the springs.[1] But not for long.

When the earliest white settlers arrived, Native Americans were pushed from the sacred springs. Most of the tribes fled or simply disappeared deep into the forests and mountains, far beyond the reach of the encroaching whites. Others, like the Utes of northwestern Colorado, fought savagely for their land. In September 1879, the Utes staged a war dance around a pile of sagebrush on which a soldier's uniform was placed. They danced for days, charging the pile of brush with their knives. Then, possessed by hatred, the Utes burned the symbolic brush pile and went off to wreak their vengeance upon the white man.[2] Not long after the resulting bloody Meeker Massacre, the Utes were forcefully removed from the springs by the United States government and relocated in unwanted tracks of land in Utah. In 1880 the Utes signed a treaty giving up all claims to land within Colorado except for a small reservation in the southwestern corner of the state.

Gradually, small villages arose around the springs of Colorado. The few Indians who remained in the area witnessed a rapidly changing culture that was vastly different from their own. From a distance they watched the construction of great pools and bathhouses. Rivers, once wild and free, were not dammed, and electric lights illuminated the night. Stagecoaches filled with elegant ladies and gentlemen rolled in from points east. Everywhere the wheels of progress were turning.

The coming of the Southern Pacific Railroad brought successive waves of easterners to the area. Railroad advertisements emphasized the state's favorable climate and reputable springs. Soon the resort towns were overrun with hopeful invalids searching for health in the clean, dry mountain air. Tent cities were erected. Then the increased commercial opportunities brought an entourage of hungry businessmen. Populations swelled. One out of every four permanent settlers in the area were health seekers. By the late nineteenth century, health resorts, which were now veritable social and cultural oases, flourished throughout the state.[3]

These were the glory days, when speculators gambled on health as a commercial industry—the days when hotel registers were replete with famous names. Everyone from the president of the United States to celebrated writers and theater stars came to Colorado to take in the waters. In 1890 Colorado boasted of more than two hundred thousand yearly visitors. Business had never been better.

But by the turn of the century, things had begun to change. The American dream that had taken root began to wither and die. Only a few of these grand old resorts survived the test of time; many were destroyed by fire, some were torn down, and others have slowly decayed. The trains don't stop anymore. Why? Who really knows the ways of fashion? Perhaps going to a health resort seems naive in a culture of miracle drugs and megavitamins; or perhaps the fact that fossil fuels are becoming scarcer and more expensive has changed our priorities. It is ironic that the very population explosion that was triggered in part by mineral springs may limit our future access to these springs. Mineral hot springs are no longer a health seeker's paradise but rather a new hope for an energy panacea.

Currently, geothermal energy is being developed in areas near hot springs, which means that eventually many springs will be tapped and some will dry up. For almost a century geologists and entrepreneurs have been exploring the possibilities of geothermal energy. Since 1904, geothermal steam has been used to generate electricity at Laradello, Italy. In ensuing years, efforts to harness this energy have been made not only in Italy but in Mexico, Japan, Iceland, New Zealand, the Soviet Union, Hungary, and of course in the United States. In Colorado, the communities of Glenwood Springs, Alamosa, Steamboat Springs, Hot Sulphur Springs, Canon City, Idaho Springs, Ouray, Salida, and Pagosa Springs have all used geothermal energy for everything from greenhouse and pool heating to fish farming and crop drying. According to the Colorado Geological Survey, the fifty-eight thermal areas in Colorado are estimated to contain energy equal to that in 490 billion tons of coal or 990 million barrels of oil.[4]

Out of the thousand hot springs in New Mexico, Idaho, California, Nevada, Wyoming, and Montana, nearly all have seen the hand of man. Today, geothermal wells are also being drilled in these areas, and this has raised the concerns of many environmentalists. For instance, some people believe that Yellowstone's geyser basin may be in grave danger if the 160 lease applications in Idaho's Targhee (a controversial geothermal area) are granted.

These hydrothermal areas may be balancing on the edge between a backwater past and a ravaged future. As economic pressures close the smaller resorts along forgotten back roads and our energy needs become more vital, our last chance to wallow in a wilderness hot tub under a star-studded midnight sky might be closer than we think. It was not supposed to be this way. Mineral water is one of the world's oldest medicines, and for thousands of years people all over the world have flocked to mineral springs seeking health; it's an ancient human tradition—a tradition that should continue until the end of time.

Descriptions of famed springs fill the pages of Greek and Roman history. The great baths of Caracalla in Rome are now legendary, but they were once authentic and surrounded by splendid gardens and statues of divinities. The Greek temples of Aesculapius—named after the god of healing, whose powers were so great that he could bring the dead back to life—were built because of the healing properties of mineral springs.[5] According to legend, many lepers bathed in these waters and were cured. Maybe these stories are highly improbable, but it is a fact that for almost five centuries the only medicines used in these ancient cultures were mineral waters. Today the water is still bottled and sold.

Gout, goiter, rheumatism, chronic bronchitis and asthma, obesity, glandular swellings, gonorrhea, hemorrhoids, headache, syphilis, scrofula, old gunshot wounds, mercurial and saturnine poisoning, rickets, menstrual and womb problems, ulcers, sore throats, back problems, muscle spasms, bunions, kidney and bladder stones, hypertrophy of the spleen and ovaries, poor digestion, and many other diseases have been cured or improved by use of mineral water, according to state geologist R. D. George.

The Japanese, having more mineral springs than any other country in the world, have traditionally believed in the regenerative and therapeutic effects of the hot mineral bath. Instead of shooting down a few fast martinis after a hard day's work, the Japanese head for the nearest public bath, where they soak their cares away. They wallow for hours in the warmth of the waters. The rich merchant talks freely with the poor rice farmer, and all social barriers evaporate like rising steam. Sometimes important business meetings are conducted in the baths. After all, without clothes it's difficult to maintain the pretensions of the business world.

In southern England, circled by an amphitheater of hills, dense forest, swamp, and spooky fog, we find the ancient city of Bath. It is an unlikely site for a city, yet magnificent shrines were built in this mysterious, misty locality by some religious cult that worshipped the healing properties of the waters. Ancient history says that the curative powers of Bath's hot springs were discovered by Bladud—King Lear's father—in the ninth century B.C. Today the baths are still used.

At one time or another, almost every country in the world has used mineral hot springs (European spas still get financial support from national governments). The most advanced societies of the Middle Ages built temples, hospitals, medical schools, and pleasure palaces around mineral springs. The Egyptians, Hebrews, and Turks never went a day without their hot soaks in luxurious pools; it was a sacred rite. The Christian sacrament of baptism, a symbol of spiritual purity, also was often administered in mineral springs.[6] And let's not forget the American aborigines, who pioneered the mineral mud bath.

Today, most of Colorado's hot-spring resorts are highly commercial, and their emphasis is on recreation rather than health. There are only a few noncommercial hot springs left that are still open to the public—the last vestiges of some sweeter time. Many hot springs aren't accessible to the public because they are located on private property. Some springs are used commercially to raise fish while others have simply dried up. Water is often skittish; it changes and shifts below the earth's surface, especially in the mountains where it is located in veins rather than in massive water tables, as it is in the East. The Colorado Geological Survey can pinpoint a certain spring on the map, and a few months later the springs water may disappear through subsurface fissures only to reappear one-half mile away.

Of all the hot springs in Colorado, only a few are too briny and hot to be considered hazardous to health. For example, the pool water at Glenwood Springs is a combination of cold springs and hot springs. If it weren't for this mixture, the water would simply be too hot for swimming.

Here is a story that exemplifies one of the potential hazards of mineral hot springs. This story was told to me by Ernie Criswell, the director of public works in the town of Salida. Ernie is a slender, graceful man with a fine, good-natured, expressive face toughened though not hardened by a life spent working mostly out-of-doors. His story goes something like this:

In the spring of 1975, Ernie was up on the hill above Poncha Springs, capping and connecting some of the twenty-one hot springs that flow by gravity five miles from Poncha Springs to fill the pool in Salida. About 11:00 A.M. he noticed a man with out-of-state plates drive up into the dirt parking lot. Ernie didn't pay much attention to him. He just remembers a bald middle-aged man going into the bathhouse instead of the outdoor pool. There wasn't anything unusual about it; people from out of state visited Poncha Springs every day. Ernie resumed working. About

1:00 P.M. he started to make his way down the hill. He was hungry as a grizzly and good and ready to go into town for lunch. The thought of meat and potatoes and biscuits all covered with gravy weighed heavily on his mind. When he reached the parking lot and was just about to hop in his county pickup truck, the caretaker of the small resort approached him and asked if he would check out the bathhouse for her. She said that the man with the out-of-state plates was still in there, and she was somewhat concerned.

With his stomach grumbling, Ernie obligingly walked to the long wooden bathhouse. As soon as he entered the building, he could feel the stifling, steamy heat. It almost took his breath away. He opened the door to the room that the man was in, and there he saw the man floating on his stomach in the six-by-six sweat bath. Ernie could see small bubbles rising around the man's head, so he thought that the man was still breathing. Still, he wasn't positive, so he stepped down on the first step of the bath. The water was deep enough to rise up over and into Ernie's boots. It was so hot that his toenails popped off almost instantly. When he reached out in the water to grab the man's arm, Ernie severely scalded his hand. He still has the scars to remember it by. The poor man who was floating in the water, which was so hot you could boil an egg in it, fell apart. As Ernie put it: "His hide peeled off as easy as the skin on a rotten grape. They literally had to take him out in a bushel basket."

Of course, this story is a little extreme, but Ernie claims that this wasn't the first time someone died in the witch's caldron at Poncha. Ernie was glad when they closed down the springs. "It wasn't a bad place for married couples and lovers," Ernie concluded, "they'll take care of one another, but unsupervised singles should never have been allowed in there."[7]

For the most part, hot springs are as safe as your own bathtub. As a matter of fact, in areas where hot springs are abundant, the local residents tell me that the wildlife tends to seek out mineral water springs for drinking water and ablution rather than the more accessible stream water.

The term "mineral water" is exact—one that includes all springs, hot or cold—for there is no such thing as "natural pure water." In most cases the water is runoff that has seeped underground through rocks, dissolving matter along the way. Some of these springs are more highly mineralized than others, and almost all springs contain large amounts of organic matter.

In the early 1800s, the explorer Zebulon Pike discovered many mineral springs throughout the West and recorded the dominant mineral content of each in his diary: arsenic, magnesium, potassium, copper, iodine, lead, and zinc.[8] It has been proven that the mineral springs of Colorado contain the therapeutic equivalent of every celebrated mineral water of Europe.

The springs that are most often praised for their therapeutic properties are thermal springs, commonly referred to as hot springs. Technically, these springs contain waters that have a temperature above the mean annual temperature of the region in which they are located. In Colorado, any springs over 45°F (7.2°C) would be considered thermal.[9]

The plains of eastern Colorado have no geothermal activity. All the hot springs are found in the Rocky Mountains and are usually quite close to recreational areas. So whether you're out running the rivers, scaling the peaks, hiking the backcountry, or horse-packing through the mountains, take that little extra side trip to one of the lesser-known hot springs. Peel off your clothes and slip your tired body into a tree-shaded hot mineral pool. Relax and watch the water as it spills over moss-covered rocks from one pool to the next. There's nothing quite like a hot soak for inducing a sense of luxury and indolence. This experience is one of a kind; not only is it good for you, but it costs very little. As you float, the soothing influence of the water unravels the knots in your mind and body. The sense of calm enjoyment and tranquility allows your thoughts to soar and drift back through time. You have a funny thought: Maybe, just maybe, Ponce de Leon was on the right track.

Notes

1. Wilson Rockwell, *The Utes—A Forgotten People* (Denver: Sage Books, 1956), pp. 21-22.
2. Josephine Meeker, *The Ute Massacre!: Brave Miss Meeker's Captivity!* (Cheyenne, Wyo.: Vic Press-Books, 1975).
3. Billy M. Jones, *Health-Seekers in the Southwest, 1817-1900* (Norman: University of Oklahoma Press, 1967), p. viii.
4. Colorado Geological Survey, *Geothermal Energy: Colorado's Untapped Resource,* Brochure no. 3104-X5 (Denver: Colorado Geological Survey, 1977).
5. Richard M. Pearl, *Springs of Colorado* (Colorado Springs: Earth Science Publishing Co., 1975), p. 4.
6. R. D. George and others, *Mineral Waters of Colorado* (Denver: Eames Brothers, State Printers, 1920), p. 36.
7. Ernie Criswell, conversation with author, June 1981.
8. Constance Brown, "But It's Always Hot-Spring Time in the Rockies," *Smithsonian* (November 1977): 94.
9. R. D. George and others, 18.

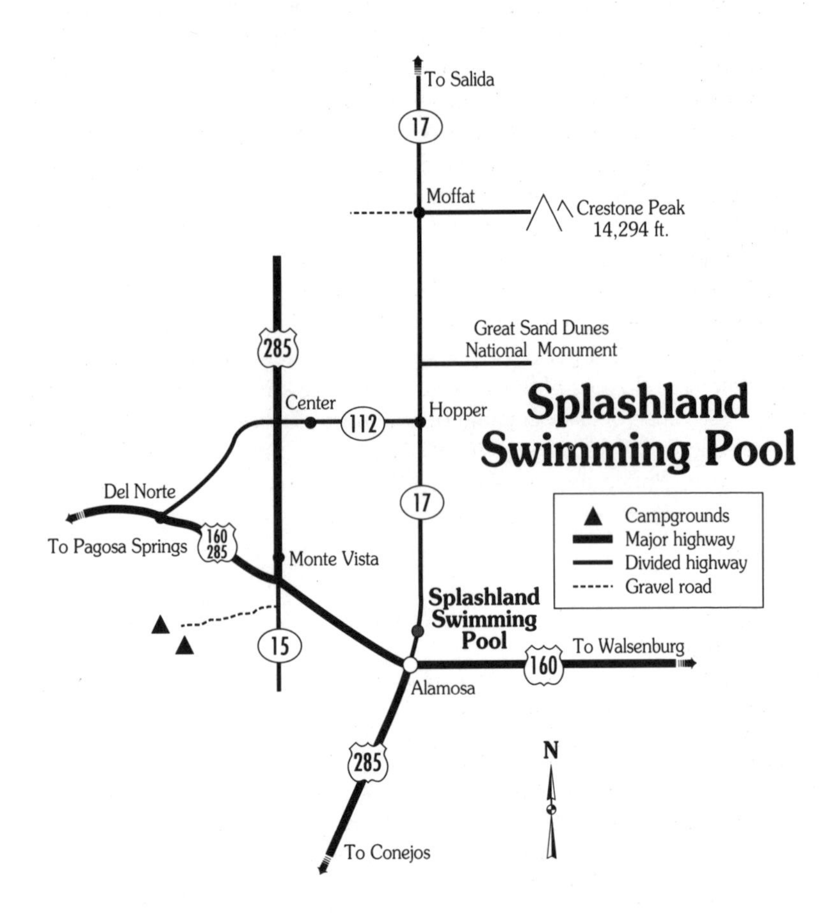
To Salida
17
Moffat
Crestone Peak
14,294 ft.
285
Great Sand Dunes
National Monument
Center
112
Hopper
Splashland
Swimming Pool
Del Norte
17
Campgrounds
Major highway
Divided highway
Gravel road
To Pagosa Springs
160
285
Monte Vista
Splashland
Swimming
Pool
15
To Walsenburg
160
Alamosa
285
N
To Conejos

Splashland Swimming Pool

Alamosa County

Splashland
Box 972
Alamosa, Colorado 81101
(303) 589-6307

Location: Route 17, 1 mile north of Alamosa
Elevation: 7,500 feet
Temperature: 87°F (41°C)
Flow: 450 gallons per minute
Services: No credit cards. Showers and locker rooms. Snack bar on premises. Open Memorial Day through Labor Day. Water from deep artesian wells supplies this large rural community swimming pool.

"Splashland is located in the center of the beautiful San Luis Valley. Some of the nation's finest potatoes and vegetable crops are grown here at this high altitude where the days are nice and warm and the nights cool." So reads a brochure describing this community plunge. It goes on to explain that two 2,000-foot free-flowing wells supply the pool. The waters contain sodium bicarbonate and have a high silica content ("a complete change over of water takes place every 8 to 10 hours").

Adjacent to the wading pool (twenty by twenty-five feet and eighteen inches deep), which is separated by a high fence to keep toddlers from straying into the adult pool (150 by 60 feet and 10 inches deep), is a grassy area with umbrella tables. Here you can sunbathe or relax with a snack.

In the distance you'll see the 14,464-foot Mount Blanca looming on the horizon. A thirty-eight-mile drive to the base of this mountain and you're at Great Sand Dunes National Monument. Splashland is rural royalty at its best!

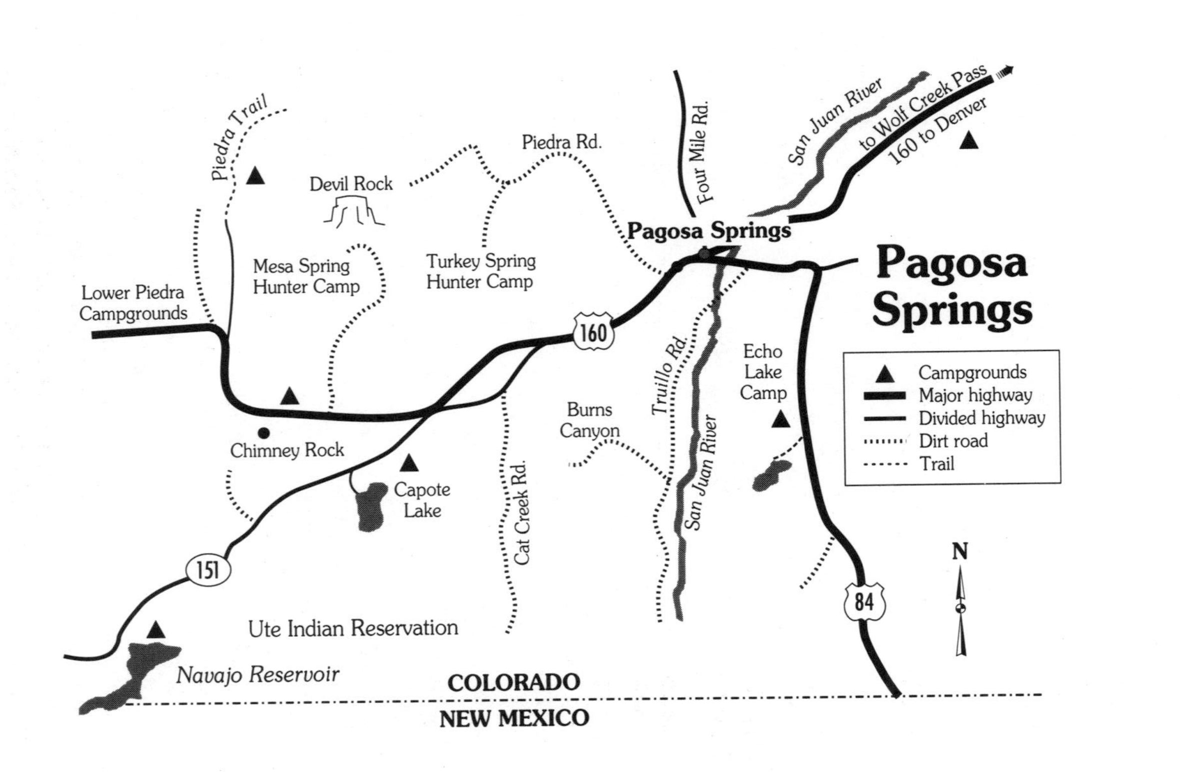
Pagosa Springs
Campgrounds
Major highway
Divided highway
Dirt road
Trail
N
Piedra Trail
Devil Rock
Piedra Rd.
Four Mile Rd.
San Juan River
to Wolf Creek Pass
160 to Denver
Pagosa Springs
Lower Piedra
Campgrounds
Mesa Spring
Hunter Camp
Turkey Spring
Hunter Camp
160
Truillo Rd.
Echo
Lake
Camp
Burns
Canyon
Chimney Rock
Capote
Lake
Cat Creek Rd.
San Juan River
151
84
Ute Indian Reservation
Navajo Reservoir
COLORADO
NEW MEXICO

Pagosa Hot Springs

Archuleta County

Location: Just off U.S. Highways 160 and 84 in the town of Pagosa Springs.
Elevation: 7,100 feet
Temperature: 133°F (56°C)
Flow: 1 million gallons per day
Services: No services on premises. All services are within walking distance. At one time these undeveloped hot springs flowed into the San Juan River, and primitive rock pools were built along the bank to facilitate bathing in the colorful muddy water.

Pagosa Springs once prospered as a health resort, but now it serves as a hunting and fishing center. Nestled in the splendor of the Rocky Mountains, the sleepy town is surrounded on the north, west, and east by San Juan National Forest and on the south by the Southern Ute Reservation.

Along Highway 160 (the old Navajo Trail) is a cluster of hot springs from which the town gets its name. According to Ute legend, the *Pagosha,* or "healing waters," were formed long before the white man when a terrible plague hit the tribe. No medicines would quench its rage. The Indians built a big fire to send a message to the Great Spirit in the sky. That night the fire turned into a boiling pool of water, and this is where the plague met its nemesis.

Possession of the springs was long disputed by the Utes and the Navajos. Finally, after a bloody battle in 1866, the springs became the undisputed property of the Utes. In 1859, a U.S. topographical engineer by the name of J. N. Macomb discovered the springs. During the Civil

War, wounded, bruised, and weary soldiers rejuvenated themselves in the hot mineral waters, and people have been soaking there ever since.

The main spring—Great Pagosa—is situated behind the Spring Inn in a basin seventy-five by sixty-five feet wide. This is the second largest spring in the state of Colorado. If you have an older guidebook, you might find a picture of a group of people frolicking in natural mud baths along the bank of a river, but this activity has been discouraged. Today the Great Pagosa Spring is fenced off from the public, and many of the other thermal springs are used to heat the town's courthouse, schools, and several business buildings. As a matter of fact, the town has received more than a million dollars in grants from the Department of Energy, and now it is considered to have one of the most successful district heating projects in the United States. But thermal energy is not new to Pagosa Springs. The townspeople have been using the hot springs for space heating ever since the turn of the century.

The outdoor enthusiast will find a rambling, rustic oasis at Pagosa Springs. There's nothing "swinging" and/or elegant about the town, except maybe New Pagosa, a condominium village just west of town. At first glance, Pagosa Springs might appear to be just another sleepy western town. But a second look reveals much more. Although Wolf Creek Pass offers some fine powder skiing, the basic tourist trade consists of hunters and fishermen, which give the town its character. The high-altitude lakes (Navajo Lake, Mullins Dam) and the hundreds of miles of clear, sparkling mountain streams offer the angler some of the best freshwater fishing in the state. In the fall, hunters will find open season on elk, deer, bighorn sheep, bear, and small game like grouse, quail, and rabbit.

There are also many other interesting diversions that are within easy driving distance: Mesa Verde National Park, Chimney Rock Archaeological Area, the Ute Indian Reservation, and the old western town of Durango. You can journey into yesteryear on the old narrow gauge railroad or take a horse-pack trip into the mountains. The surrounding national forest offers camping and hiking at its best (the Continental Divide Trail can be found in the area).

Pagosa Hot Springs

Archuleta County

Spring Inn
165 Hot Spring Boulevard
Pagosa Springs, Colorado 81147
(303) 262-2287

(See map on page 12.)

Summer or winter, this twenty-one room inn is one of the most delightful hot-spring resorts in Colorado. With four outdoor Jacuzzi spas on a closed-in deck, and a hot-spring pool overlooking the San Juan River, this is a peaceful place to relax and view a Rocky Mountain sunset. All rooms are thermally heated and are furnished with color cable TV.

Next door, a store offers mountain bike rentals and winter ski packages. The Wolf Creek Ski Area is fast becoming one of the premier ski resorts in the state. With the area's average of five hundred inches of snow a year, you'll find some of Colorado's finest powder and most spectacular scenery.

Bars, cafes, and family eateries are all within walking distance, and the river walk, complete with descriptive signs, is a perfect place to take a stroll and learn about the history and geology of the area. Pagosa Springs has made a commitment to improving its hot springs and hot-spring experience, and it is destined to become one of the state's top spas.

Pagosa Hot Springs

Archuleta County

The Spa
Box 37
Pagosa Springs, Colorado 81147
(303) 264-5910

(See map on page 12.)

Entering downtown Pagosa Springs from the north on U.S. 160, you'll notice an old bridge built across the San Juan River on the east side of the road. Drive across it and you're at The Spa.

Although today's doctors take a mixed view of spa therapy, the Spa Motel still advertises its therapeutic mineral pool and sweat baths. There are two separate bathhouses—men's and women's—in which bathing suits aren't required. These are open to the public for a small fee; however, the outdoor pool is reserved for motel guests only.

Although the resort is open year-round, summer is the most popular season, peaking in July with Red Ryder Days. But the action is too sedate to draw the chic set; like many Colorado watering places, The Spa appeals to a conservative, family clientele.

The accommodations range from units with light housekeeping facilities to regular motel rooms. If you tend to overextend yourself on vacations, at least do it where a cure is near at hand. Here you can soak in the carbo-gaseous baths, which are very good for heart disease, high blood pressure, and hardening of the arteries. All services are available in the town of Pagosa Springs.

The Spa in Pagosa Springs.

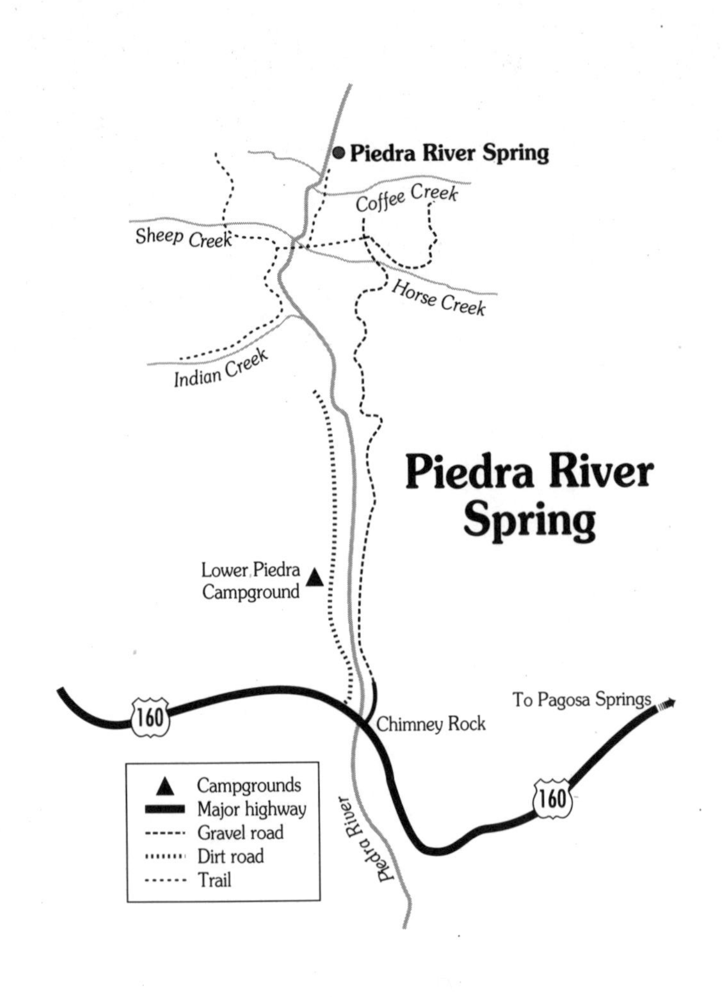

Piedra River Spring
Coffee Creek
Sheep Creek
Horse Creek
Indian Creek
Piedra River Spring
Lower Piedra
Campground
160
Chimney Rock
To Pagosa Springs
160
Campgrounds
Major highway
Gravel road
Dirt road
Trail
Piedra River

Piedra River Spring

Archuleta County

Location: West of Chimney Rock to the forest access road running north along the east bank of the Piedra River, then 6.7 miles to Sheep Creek Trail. The springs extend for approximately thirty yards along the shore and may be submerged during high-water seasons.
Elevation: 6,540 feet
Temperature: 97°F (42°C)
Flow: 50 gallons per minute
Services: Camping

Piedra River Spring lies toward the center of the southern reaches of Colorado and is one of the most primitive springs in the state—seldom used by people and often used by forest critters.

To reach the spring, travel west of Chimney Rock on U.S. 160 (approximately three miles) until you reach the first forest access road running north along the east bank of the Piedra River. Here, just before U.S. 160 crosses the Piedra River, is where you turn off.

First Fork Road winds for twelve miles along the river, taking you deep into the lush wilderness of the San Juan National Forest, and eventually ends at a campground. About halfway up the road (approximately 6.7 miles) you'll come to the intersection of Monument Park Road and First Fork Road. This is where Sheep Creek Trail begins, which will lead you toward the springs.

The trail cuts downward steeply for approximately one-half mile, then the valley floor widens into a beautiful parklike meadow carpeted with clover. In the distance you'll see a steel-cabled bridge for horses that spans the gleaming waters of the river. If you're a fisherman, this convenient wilderness amenity allows you to fish both sides of the river. But if you're trying to locate the springs, you won't have to cross the bridge. You'll take the First Fork Trail north (one mile) through the woods until you reach Coffee Creek. At this point you'll see numerous animal trails zigzagging down through another meadow toward the river and the springs. Deer and elk are especially fond of the sodium water; birds, coyotes, even bears are attracted to the small pools. You, too, can slake your thirst and fill up your canteen here, but the water is not as palatable to humans as it seems to be to woodland creatures.

These springs aren't used much for bathing; the abundance of animal scat around the springs is usually enough to deter would-be skinny-dippers. Not only that, but during the high-water season the springs are usually submerged. Even if the river isn't running high, the springs may be plugged with silt and the flow may be impeded.

The closest town to the Piedra campground is Chimney Rock (named after a geological formation that resembles, you guessed it, a chimney). Close by you'll find the Chimney Rock Archaeological Area, undoubtedly the most educational entertainment around. When you're in town you might want to stop at Chimney Rock Restaurant for breakfast or go next door to the Pint Jar Bar for beer and nachos while you watch the football game on TV. For your convenience, a small liquor store and a game-processing shed are on the premises. That's about all there is to Chimney Rock. For more action and a better variety of restaurants, you'll have to travel a few miles east to Pagosa Springs.

Piedra River Spring is a place to bring your tent and fishing pole, a place where the lone backpacker can set up camp, fish, and enjoy the best of the great outdoors. Here, in this leafy solitude, you can build a crackling campfire at twilight, prepare yourself a boiling pot of pine needle tea, and sit back and wait for the forest creatures to come to the springs and drink.

Eldorado Warm Springs

Boulder County

Eldorado Artesian Springs
P.O. Box 445
Eldorado Springs, Colorado 80025
(303) 499-1316

Location: Five miles south of Boulder on Highway 93 to Eldorado Springs turnoff, then west three miles. Next to Eldorado Canyon State Park.
Elevation: 5,600 feet
Temperature: 77°F (25°C)
Flow: 10-15 gallons per minute. Total discharge, 160 gallons per minute
Services: No credit cards. Excellent walking trails, mountain-stream fishing, climbing, horseback riding, creekside picnic area, twenty tent sites (no electricity), snack bar with hot dogs and soda and such. Ballroom with bar and fireplace, which can be rented for special occasions. Holistic seminars. Open June to November.

Eldorado Springs, at the mouth of South Boulder Canyon, is one of the earliest resorts in the state. Around the turn of the century it was considered the eye of the social and cultural hurricane. Then it hit a streak of bad luck. In 1929 a fire swept through the resort, causing $150,000 in damages. The owners rebuilt, but on Labor Day in 1938 a flood raged through the canyon, destroying most of the buildings. Again the resort was rebuilt, only to be devastated by another fire in 1939. But somehow the resort always seemed to retain its popularity. Today the resort is back in operation. Ever since Eldorado Canyon State Park opened in 1978, the

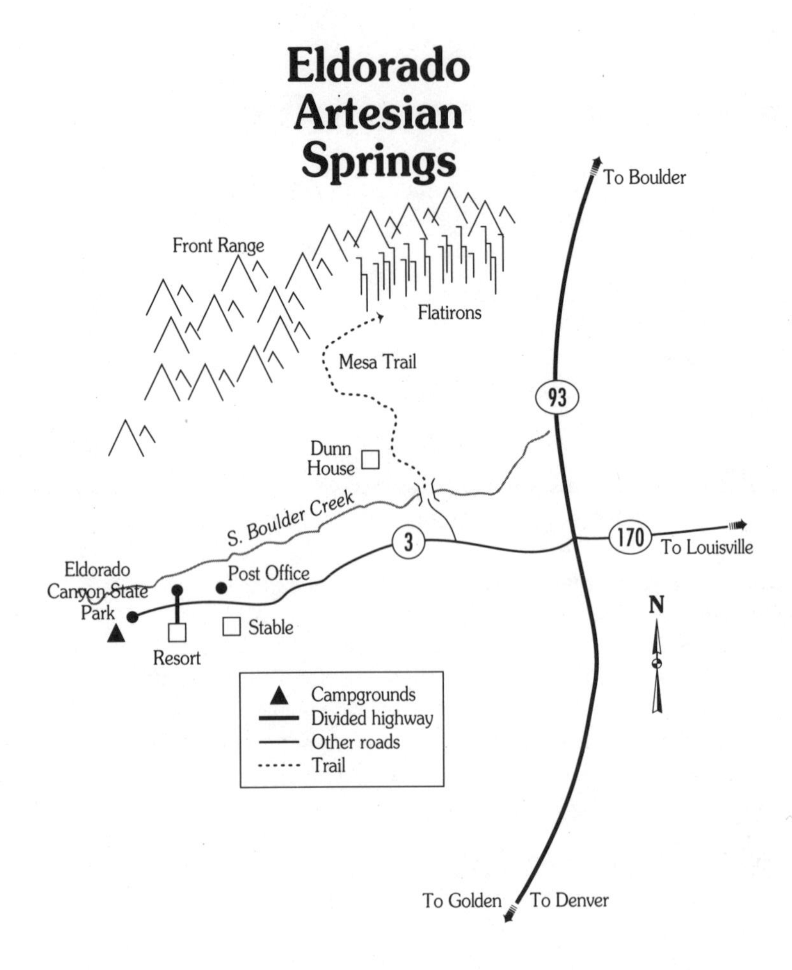
Eldorado
Artesian
Springs
To Boulder
Front Range
Flatirons
Mesa Trail
93
Dunn
House
S. Boulder Creek
170
To Louisville
3
Eldorado
Canyon State
Park
Post Office
Stable
Resort
N
Campgrounds
Divided highway
Other roads
Trail
To Golden
To Denver

resort has attracted as many as two thousand visitors a week. Many come to swim in the artesian swimming pool. Others are technical climbers who come to scale the world-famous canyon walls. And still others come to hike, to ride horses, to fish, to camp, and to take in the splendor of it all.

About a mile before you reach the little canyon town, on the right side of the road you'll see a solitary two-story brick building out in a field on the far side of the creek. A parking and picnic area is located here. This is also where the Mesa Trail begins. It will lead you to the old Dunn House—one of the first homesteads in the Eldorado area, settled in 1860. The trail winds through an open meadow toward the Front Range and eventually leads you into the town of Boulder. This is a good cross-country ski trail.

As you enter Eldorado Springs from the east, you first pass the post office—a one-room white clapboard building on the right side of the road. Across the street is a small stable where you can rent horses by the hour; it opens Memorial Day. If you're a romantic at heart, you might want to check out the moonlight rides.

Your first impression of Eldorado Springs—drawn from all the old cars parked along the road—might be that this is where retired Volvos come to die. But your impression will change. Farther down the road you'll see the old resort and a bunch of rustic cabins scattered along the creek and hillsides. To almost anybody, Eldorado would look like a summer retreat for people who like the out-of-doors. It's not really a resort town; there are no gift shops, boutiques, restaurants, or beauty parlors here. It's just a nice place to swim—either in the creek or in the swimming pool—and enjoy a picnic. I like to come here after the season has ended, when the pool is empty and the local residents have gone into hibernation. It's a nice quiet place to take a short hike and get away from the hustle and bustle of the city.

During the summer season you can stand on the floor of the canyon and look up at a few dozen or more lonely little figures clinging by their fingernails to the sides of the sheer canyon walls. For years now people have been coming from all over the world with their ropes, rivets, and hammers to take on these magnificent rock formations with heroic names like Wind Tower, Holy Cross, Bastille, and Naked Edge. The climbing is so good here that it has even attracted the attention of *Life* magazine and *Wide World of Sports;* after all, climbing can be a great spectator sport.

It all started in 1902, when the Union Pacific and Moffat Railroad was built above the valley. Two years later the Moffat Lakes Resort Company,

The Eldorado Springs resort in the 1920s. *(Courtesy Eldorado Historical Society)*

consisting of Frank Fowler and three partners, purchased the land. The next year, 1905, the first summer resort in Colorado was opened. This was Frank Fowler's dream. In 1908 he built a forty-room hotel. It was a romantic creation, with white pillars and a sweeping veranda where people could sit in rocking chairs and look out over South Boulder Creek. That same year, the Denver Interurban Railway was connected, and before long, hundreds of urban cowboys were coming to the springs (round-trip fare was $1.50). The resort was advertised as the "Coney Island of Colorado."

Who Is That Daring Young Man?

Each summer season would open with spectacular feats of wire-balancing. Ivy Baldwin, a daredevil, balloonist, and trapeze artist, would walk a three-eighths-inch cable across the mouth of the canyon, 635 feet above the tumbling white waters of the creek. In the middle of his journey, he excited crowds by standing on his head while the cable swayed in the gusty canyon wind. Ivy crossed South Boulder Creek eighty-eight

Daredevil Ivy Baldwin crossing South Boulder Canyon. *(Courtesy Eldorado Historical Society)*

times—the last time on his eighty-second birthday. He continued to live in the canyon as a guest of the Fowlers until his peaceful death at the age of eighty-seven in 1953.

Ivy loved it here, but then again, anyone who enters the canyon usually falls in love with it. Ike and Mamie Eisenhower chose this scenic spot for their honeymoon in 1916; others, like Walter Winchell, John Barrymore, Jimmy Durante, and Jack Dempsey, all came here for fun and relaxation. The canyon makes for instant memories. The Fowlers say that it is blessed.

Among all the peole who have come to know and cherish this canyon, none loved it more than the Utes. They believed the springs and the canyon to be enchanted. When the winter snows began to fly, the people of this mountain tribe probably strapped their tepee poles to their horses and tracked their game along the creek, fishing for trout and gathering edible roots and berries until they reached the springs. Here the steep canyon walls protected and comforted them during the hard winters.

The name Eldorado (Spanish for "golden one") summons up images of ancient explorers and cities of gold. One might guess that the Spanish conquistadors named the canyon because of the yellow ochre color of the lichen-tinged walls that changes subtly in the shifting canyon light. Actually, Frank Fowler named the area in 1902. For him the name was full of grandeur and whimsy; it meant "a pot of gold at the end of the rainbow."

Back in the 1920s, when the springs were called Boulder Radium Springs, the large outdoor pool and dance hall were the main attractions. The health seekers of the day believed that the high radium content of these waters exerted potent therapeutic effects. After the fire of 1929, which took thirteen cabins and all the buildings except the hotel, the resort was almost immediately rebuilt, but this time, pavilions, shooting galleries, a new dance hall, and balconies were built around the pool. On summer weekends, hundreds of people hiked the "Crazy Stairs"—1,350 steps—to the top of the Bastille to have their picnics. The view was stunning from up there. You could see forever. You could also look down at the resort and watch the swimmers and roller skaters in the roller rink; and best of all, if you were lucky, you could hear Glenn Miller's jazz trombone echoing in the canyon.

Today the spring-fed pool is considered to have the lowest mineral content of any springs in the United States. Although this makes for some of the most comfortable swimming water in the state of Colorado, nobody

Eldorado Artesian Springs today.

is much concerned about the therapeutic effects. Even the names of the springs—Currie, Cave, Bath, and Arapahoe—are seldom, if ever, mentioned anymore.

People have always felt something magical, mystical, and spiritual in the canyon. In Eldorado there is a sense of history, of time and of place. It's not terribly difficult to imagine Glenn Miller striking up his orchestra in the crowded ballroom, or Jack Dempsey reeling in a trout for breakfast, or even the handsome army officer and his new bride taking a moonlight stroll in the canyon. Eldorado is so full of good things: adventure, romance, and the music of the swallows darting in the canyon. It's a virtual paradise. Although there is no more jazz music in the ballroom, and the Crazy Stairs and Ivy Baldwin's high wire have long since been torn down, the essence of the canyon will never change.

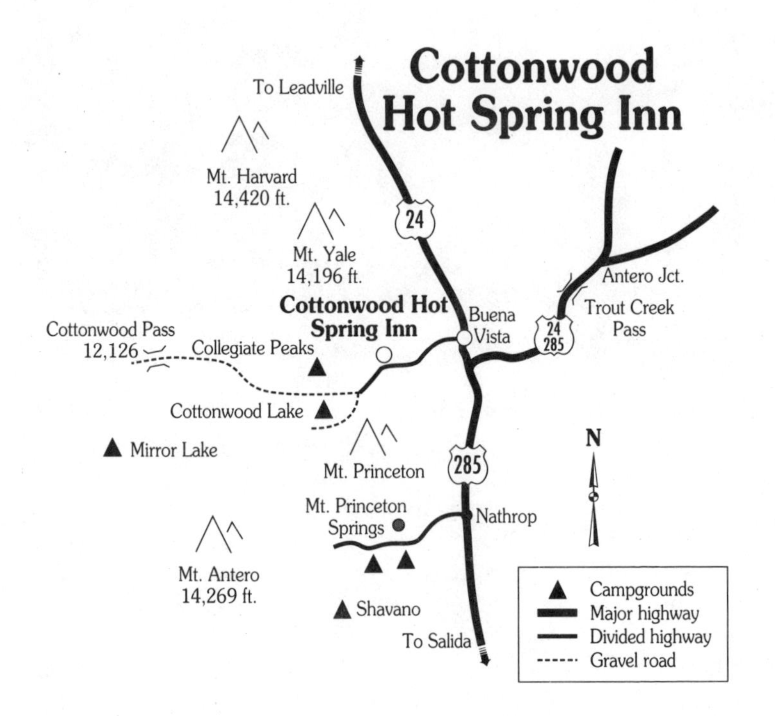
Cottonwood Hot Spring Inn
To Leadville
Mt. Harvard
14,420 ft.
24
Mt. Yale
14,196 ft.
Cottonwood Hot Spring Inn
Buena Vista
Antero Jct.
Trout Creek Pass
24
285
Cottonwood Pass
12,126
Collegiate Peaks
Cottonwood Lake
Mirror Lake
Mt. Princeton
285
N
Mt. Princeton Springs
Nathrop
Mt. Antero
14,269 ft.
Shavano
To Salida
Campgrounds
Major highway
Divided highway
Gravel road

Cottonwood Hot Springs

Chaffee County

Cottonwood Hot Spring Inn (Jump Steady Resort)
18999 Highway 306
Buena Vista, Colorado
(719) 395-6434

Location: Six miles west of Buena Vista on State Highway 306, along the bank of Cottonwood Creek
Elevation: 7,954 feet
Temperature: 129°F (54°C)
Flow: 110 gallons per minute
Services: Visa and MasterCard accepted. Twelve rooms and three cabins. Open year-round.

Of all the hot springs in Colorado, few conjure up the nostalgic images of the Old West the way Jump Steady Resort does. It reminds me of an old Hollywood movie set, where I wouldn't be surprised to see Miss Kitty and Matt Dillon scuffling their heels along the wooden sidewalk. This western resort was built in 1966, but it has changed owners a few times since then, and each time it changes hands, the motif of the place changes, too.

Today the motel bathrooms and three outdoor hydrojet hot tubs are all supplied with mineral water. A word of caution: Only *really hot* water flows from the faucets. The owner suggests that showers be taken early in the morning, when the water is coolest. Otherwise, you have to fill the tub and let the water cool.

The resort has always been a popular attraction for the residents of Buena Vista. The Jump Steady Bar and Restaurant, creekside cabins, and hot mineral water (so soothing you'll want to soak forever) are among the specialties on this resort's menu. There's a woodsy, friendly atmosphere here in an area that needs more places like this. Exercise facilities and massage by appointment are also available.

Situated at the mouth of Cottonwood Canyon, the resort is a perfect retreat for the hunter and the angler. The surrounding San Isabel National Forest shelters every type of big game indigenous to Colorado, and Cottonwood Creek and Cottonwood Lake (five miles away) offer splendid trout fishing.

The Jump Steady Resort is just down the road from where the old Cottonwood Resort Hotel once stood. The spectacular bicycle races from Buena Vista to the springs were once known throughout Colorado. It was the nineteenth-century version of the Coors Classic. But fate put a curse on the hotel—in 1885 it was destroyed in a terrible fire. An article from the *Buena Vista Democrat* (July 15, 1885) reported the sad event: "This disaster is a bad blow to our town for present. The Springs were becoming notoriously famous and loads of visitors were enjoying the blessings of its waters. It is but a short time when a new Hotel will be built." It was rebuilt, but in 1911 the owner burned the grand old hotel to the ground in hopes of collecting insurance money. This time the hotel was never rebuilt, and the bicycle races were discontinued. Today the people at the Jump Steady Resort are trying to revive the spirit of the glory days.

Mount Princeton Hot Springs

Chaffee County

Mount Princeton Hot Spring Resort
15870 County Road 162
Nathrop, Colorado 81236
(719) 395-2447

Location: U.S. 285 to Route 162, then five miles west to the resort
Elevation: 8,500 feet
Temperature: 111° to 135°F (44° to 57°C)
Flow: 315 gallons per minute
Services: The resort offers rooms, a spacious dining room, and a picnic area. Camping, horseback riding, fishing, skiing, hiking, white-water raft trips, and jeep rides are also available. No credit cards. Open all year.

Surrounded by the San Isabel National Forest, Mount Princeton is one of the most beautiful hot-spring resorts in the state. It is located about one-half hour's drive from Salida. The snow-covered peaks of Shavano, Antero, Princeton, Yale, and Columbia tower above 14,000 feet to the west in the rugged Sawatch Range. Chalk Creek (so named because of the powdery color of the claylike canyon cliffs) rushes by the outdoor swimming pool, which is maintained at 95°F (35°C). Another large mineral pool is located across from the lodge. The bathhouse contains six private indoor tubs that are maintained at 110°F (43.3°C). Bathing suits are required in the outdoor pool areas.

The best and quickest way for a visitor to get a dramatic impression of the scope and rich history of the Mount Princeton area would be to take a drive west of the resort to the old ghost town of St. Elmo. At the

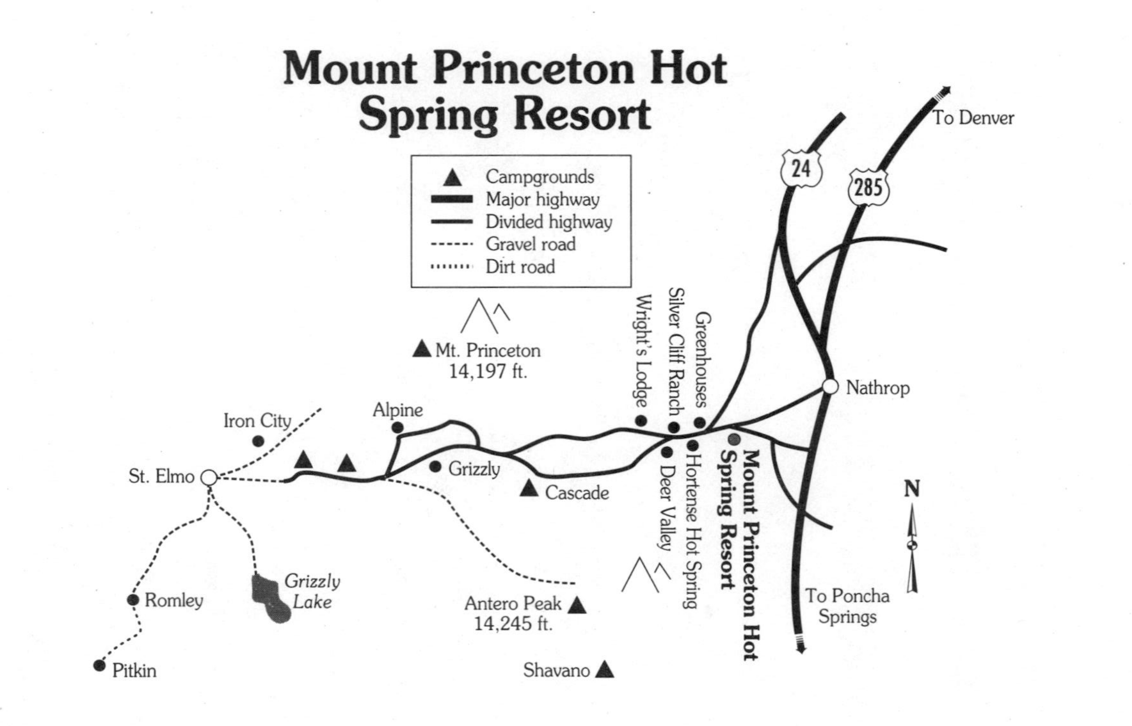
Mount Princeton Hot
Spring Resort
Campgrounds
Major highway
Divided highway
Gravel road
Dirt road
To Denver
24
285
Nathrop
Greenhouses
Silver Cliff Ranch
Wright's Lodge
Mount Princeton Hot
Spring Resort
Hortense Hot Spring
Deer Valley
Mt. Princeton
14,197 ft.
Alpine
Iron City
St. Elmo
Grizzly
Cascade
N
To Poncha
Springs
Grizzly
Lake
Romley
Pitkin
Antero Peak
14,245 ft.
Shavano

The Mount Princeton Hot Springs resort and Hotel Antero in the 1920s. *(Courtesy Colorado Historical Society)*

height of the mining boom, fifty mines were operating in the Chalk Creek area and towns like this were popping up everywhere. But the mines didn't produce as much gold as was hoped, and many towns were abandoned.

Mount Princeton survived, but it has gone through some radical changes. The Utes, who used to winter in the warm thermal caves along the creek, disappeared when the first white men entered the valley. In 1860, miners built a two-story log building by the site of the springs. In 1879, construction began on one of Colorado's grandest resort hotels, the Hotel Antero. By 1880 the Denver, South Park and Pacific Railroad chugged over the mountain peaks. More and more people were arriving each day, yet the hotel wasn't completed until forty years later. It was a plush creation, even by European standards. Large balconies looked out over well-kept gardens.

But the glory days were gone in a flash. The railroad and all the mining operations were shut down by 1925. The 1930s brought the Depression and with it a declining interest in health spas. Although the hotel had 100 rooms and cost more than $75,000, it was never a financial success. The elegant ballroom and croquet lawns were only reminders of the way things once were. The building was dismantled in 1950. It took a Texas construction company just five months to salvage what had taken nearly half a century to create.[1]

There are many springs in the Mount Princeton group. Heywood Spring (named after a government surveyor who purchased the property in the 1860s), Big Spring, Hotel Spring, and Hayes' Iron Spring have all been tapped in order to supply the pools and water the lawns. One mile west of Mount Princeton is Hortense Spring (once the site of a boom town), which is the hottest spring in the state, at 165° to 183°F (74° to 84°C). Wright Spring is used to heat a private greenhouse.

As I drove up to the springs early one spring morning, I saw a small herd of mule deer. A red-tailed hawk soared high above, and a snowshoe rabbit bounced across the road. "What a great place," I thought to myself, "to have a hot-spring hideaway."

Notes

1. Don Smith, *Chalk Creek to the Past* (privately printed, 1958), p. 11.

Poncha Hot Springs

Chaffee County

Location: Five miles west of the town of Salida on U.S. 50. Turn south at Junction 285. Take the first road after the bridge. Turn left and follow the road, keeping to the right; the dirt road takes you to the springs.
Elevation: 7,250 feet
Temperature: 133° to 158°F (56° to 70°C)
Flow: 135 gallons per minute combined flow of all springs
Services: None. The Camp Fire Girls have a summer lease; anyone else who wishes to use the springs must be granted permission by the town of Poncha Springs.

Poncha Springs—originally called Poncho Springs—is set along a mountain slope from which bubble forty-five hot mineral springs. The early settlers of Poncha realized the positive economic effect that these springs could have on their growing community. An article in the *Rocky Mountain News,* dated August 28, 1879, pointed out this fact: "Through the season the visitors have averaged from 15 to 20 per day, but as there were no accommodations they passed on . . . Next spring a hotel is to be erected near the springs, on a plateau just below, sufficiently large to accommodate 200 to 300 and other improvements made, which the wants of a fashionable visiting population require."

Eventually, a three-story frame building was erected near the springs, one mile above the town of Poncha. An early prospectus advertised: "These springs are the greatest natural attractions of the world-famous mountain scenery of Colorado, and they cannot fail . . . to bring thousands of travelers and tourists to Poncha." And so the tourists came, and the little town of Poncha became a major spa. Then, late one

September night in 1903, the hotel burned to the ground. Although the hotel was never rebuilt, the spa continued to operate for many more years. But after a fatal accident in 1975 in which a tourist was boiled alive in one of the sweat baths, the local health department closed it down. Now the bathhouse is slowly decaying.

Poncho, an Indian word for "tobacco," was the name given to the town and the springs by Joe Hartuck, who once successfully grew tobacco here.

Although the springs are no longer for public use, the water is collected in large cement pools and piped down from the mountains to Salida, five miles away. The mineral water arrives at an indoor pool at a pleasant 114°F (45.5°C).

Salida Hot Springs

Chaffee County

Salida Hot Springs Pool
410 West Rainbow Boulevard
Salida, Colorado 81201
(719) 539-6738

Location: Six miles west of U.S. 285 on U.S. 50 in the town of Salida
Elevation: 7,000 feet
Temperature: Pool maintained at 70°F (21.1°C). Baths maintained at 117° to 120°F (47.2° to 48.8°C).
Flow: Mineral water piped from Poncha Springs
Services: No credit cards. RV spaces and picnic grounds on premises; tennis courts, volleyball courts, and horseshoe pits. One mile to public golf course. Open all year.

The story of Salida (Spanish for "gateway") is really a tale of two cities, for without the water supplied by Poncha Springs, five miles away, there would be no mineral-water pool and sweat baths at Salida.

The renovated swimming pool was completed in the summer of 1981. It was once an outdoor pool, but with the new construction a roof was added. Video games, pinball machines, and a jukebox were also installed. An upper deck outside of the pool area can be used for sunbathing. Six modern indoor sweat baths are available for families and couples. A comfy cot is also supplied for those who feel that it's necessary (and it usually is necessary) to take a nap after such a luxurious soak. Bathing suits are required in the pool area.

The gold rush of 1860 brought the first white settlers to the valley (unlucky gold rushers were attracted by the fertile farmland of Salida). At this time there were as many as eight stages running through the valley between Canon City and Leadville. In 1880 the railroad finally reached Salida. The construction of a mineral-water pool was still a distant dream.

When Salida finally succeeded in piping the water from Poncha Springs to the city, it was one of the most memorable occasions in the history of the valley. Although the work on the pipeline started in 1935, it progressed slowly, and it wasn't until 1938 that the pool was opened. An article from the *Salida Daily Mail,* dated June 23, 1938, recaptures that joyous day: "There were grumblings that the project was 'Mayor Ferno's Folly,' but when finally the building was erected and the water turned in, and the beautiful subsurface lights turned on, there was nothing but the highest praise." The article went on to say: "The old time residents of Salida always maintained that the bringing of the water to Salida would make the city's future secure." Today the city's future *is* secure. The pool and baths attract many tourists because the waters are curative and widely known. The people of Salida are proud of their pool, and they have a right to be.

If it's spectacular scenery you want, Salida has it. You can see nine mountain peaks from Salida, all over 14,000 feet high. Mounts Ouray, Shavano, and Antero were named after three Ute chiefs whose tribes were among the first to cross the upper Arkansas River Valley. The so-called Collegiate Peaks—Harvard, Princeton, and Yale—also stand as stately as their names against the sky. Any one of these mountains would be a challenge to an experienced backpacker or climber. One of the best scenic drives in the area will take you up a spiral road to Tenderfoot Mountain, which rises 500 feet above Salida and offers a spectacular wraparound view of the Arkansas River Valley.

Although the buffalo no longer roam the high valley, and the Indians, Spaniards, and fur trappers have gone the way of yesterday's memories, Salida still remains a gateway to fun and pleasure. It may not stand up to the expectations of a sophisticated world traveler, but if you're looking for a low-key place to relax and a great place to swim and bathe, this is it. (See Poncha Springs, on page 35.)

Idaho Hot Springs

Clear Creek County

Indian Springs Resort
302 Soda Creek Road
Idaho Springs, Colorado 80452
Local: (303) 567-2191
Denver: (303) 623-2050

Location: Take Interstate 70 to Idaho Springs exit, then follow the signs to Soda Springs Road
Elevation: 7,500 feet
Temperature: 68° to 115°F (20° to 46°C)
Flow: 50 gallons per minute
Services: Visa and MasterCard accepted. Thirty-two rooms, live music weekends, geothermal tunnels, indoor and outdoor baths and pools, Swedish massage, tennis and volleyball courts, horseshoe pits, archery range, campground.

A little more than a century ago, the town of Idaho Springs was nothing more than an Indian reservation; a few years later, when gold and silver were discovered, it became one of the most important cities of the West. What makes the area (a one-hour drive from Denver) worthwhile now is the single most magnificent resort site on this planet. Surrounded by the alpine glory of Arapaho National Forest, the Indian Springs Resort boasts the finest hot springs in the state. There is a large swimming pool covered with a translucent dome and filled with naturally hot mineral water. Enclosed with the pool is part of the mountain and a splendid flower garden that provides a springtime setting year-round. But the most unique features of this resort are the geothermal tunnels that are located

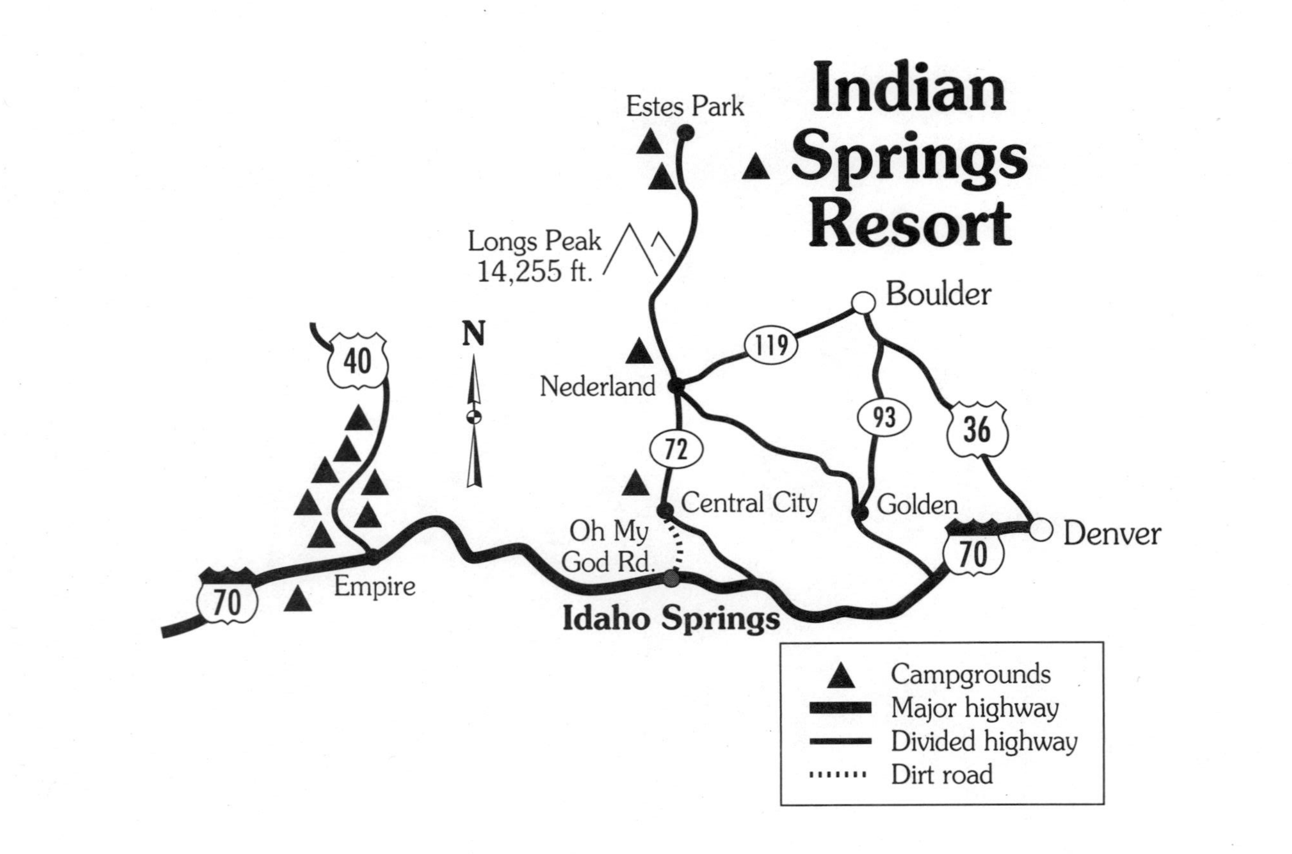
Indian
Springs
Resort
Estes Park
Longs Peak
14,255 ft.
Boulder
N
40
Nederland
119
93
36
72
Central City
Golden
Denver
Oh My
God Rd.
70
Empire
70
Idaho Springs
Campgrounds
Major highway
Divided highway
Dirt road

underneath the hotel. For skiers traveling to and from the nine large ski areas that are all within easy driving distance, a visit to these hot caverns is guaranteed to evoke a sense of serene opulence that is not available elsewhere. For those who like to eat and drink, a two-block walk to the center of town will reveal a galaxy of low-rent bars and funky cafes. (Miner Street is considered the Restaurant Row of Idaho Springs.)

Best of all available diversions is the scenic drive up the highest auto road in the United States to the top of Mount Evans. On the way up to the 14,260-foot peak, you'll pass Echo Lake and Summit Lake, two great picnicking spots. And if you're a western history buff, you'll find several gold mines to tour (Argo is the biggest and the best), plus mining museums.

The first time I visited the resort I took a shortcut from Central City to Idaho Springs. The old gravel stagecoach road is icy in January (perhaps that is why someone named it "Oh My God Road"), but I figured if the stagecoach could make this trip thrice-weekly back in 1867, I certainly could make it with no problem today. Although the road is better maintained now than it was back then, and modern luxuries—like shock absorbers—make the going a little easier, I still wouldn't recommend this road after a heavy snow. Any other time, it's a fun road to drive, winding through some of the most famous gold-mining country in the state and past the once-thriving boom town of Russel Gulch. There are still many active mines along this road, but mostly I noticed old abandoned mines peppering the landscape (Caution: these old mine shafts are extremely dangerous). When I finally made it up through the pass and began to descend toward town, I got my first glimpse of the Indian Springs Resort. I could just barely see the historic hotel through the towering pines, nestled in a mountain valley along Soda Creek.

Fifteen minutes later I found myself in the hotel dining room (aptly named the Victorian Lounge and Restaurant), engaged in a leisurely conversation with an older couple seated nearby. The old gent did most of the talking. He had a weathered face and wore a western shirt and faded jeans. He was a tough old rancher from southern Colorado, and he had been coming to the resort once a month for the last thirty years, ever since he had developed severe arthritis in his hands at the age of fifty. He said that by soaking one or two days a month in the mineral baths, he could go back to his ranch near Pueblo and get kicked by his cows until the next month rolled around; then he was ready for the mineral baths again. His wife said that it was all in his head, and I almost believed

The Indian Hot Springs Resort in Idaho Springs.

her. But then I remembered the miraculous testimonials that were posted in the hotel lobby. Knowing the abuse that my body has suffered through the years, I wanted to head straight for the baths, determined on purification. However, a stirring in the pit of my stomach brought something more immediate to mind. I ordered the luncheon special—spaghetti. Mamma Celeste would have considered the meal a sacrilege, but the price was right—under two dollars, including a trip to the salad bar.

While I waited for my meal to arrive, I asked the old man about the band equipment in the small barroom. He told me that a "hellzapoppin" country group played in there three times a week. He said that it got really wild sometimes, especially on Thursday nights when free country-swing dance lessons were given.

After coffee, the old rancher offered to take me on a tour of the resort. Except for a few coats of paint, I would have guessed that the resort hadn't changed much since Frank and Jesse James signed the hotel register. Ruby red Victorian lamps hung from the ceiling, and the small restrooms still only accommodate one person at a time.

We might have been walking into antiquity as we entered the mineral baths and found ourselves in a misty underground cavern buried deep in the side of Santa Fe Mountain. These dimly lit caves conjure up spooky images of another world. But this is not the way it really is. The way it is—a world emphasizing health and fitness—includes everyone from arthritic grandmothers to tired skiers. There are separate tunnels for men and women, and although bathing suits are prohibited in the tunnels, they are required in the swimming area.

Down a dank hallway is a series of vaultlike rooms, all with walls and floors of red stone and all lighted by small bare white bulbs. These cubicles contain private sweat baths that are available to couples and families. The mineral water used here is considered among the finest in the world. A 1976 government analysis proved that all twelve trace minerals required for good health are present in these waters.

The old rancher told me how the caves were discovered. The story dated back to 1859, when George Jackson discovered gold on Chicago Creek. The word spread, and the rush to the Rockies was on. One hundred thousand easterners beat a path across the dusty plains that year shouting "Pike's Peak or Bust." Four thousand of these men came to Idaho Springs to seek their fortunes at "Jackson's diggings." They dynamited and tunneled into the innards of the earth, but only a few struck pay dirt. Two unlucky miners burrowed into the side of a mountain only

The Ocean Bath House in 1880. *(Courtesy Colorado Historical Society)*

to discover a hot-water mine. It was a bust to the two miners but a boon to the town of Idaho Springs, for this tunnel gave birth to the Indian Springs Resort.

As the name suggests, Indian Springs was first used by the Indians. Unlike the other springs of Colorado, these springs were not only used by the Utes but also by the Arapaho, who inadvertently gave their name to the present town, *Edah hoe,* meaning "gem of the mountains." It was a name that spoke truth, for this was a land of peace, a sacred land where any tribe was allowed to bring its sick and wounded to be healed by the waters of the Great Spirit.

Soon after the two unlucky miners sold their land, a little log cabin was built near the hot water mine (Ocean Bath House). The Indians watched from a distance as their hunting grounds were overrun with hordes of white men and their streams were poisoned with mine tailings. They saw their game driven east to the plains, and then they, too, rode off into the sunset—never to return.

Through the years, ownership of the springs traded hands several times, and each time it was traded, more and more improvements were made. By 1880 it was considered one of the nation's most fashionable resorts. Between 1924 and 1931, over $300,000 was spent renovating what was then called the Radium Hot Springs. The old rancher told me that the resort had so much class that Billy the Kid and Sarah Bernhardt stayed here. At first I wondered if he meant that they stayed together, but then he mentioned other notables like Walt Whitman, the Vanderbilts, and the Roosevelts. It seemed like an unlikely gathering. Yet the resort remains much the same as it was in the thirties, and although the name has been changed, it still attracts thousands of visitors each year.

At dusk, I headed back toward home. As the old stagecoach road rose through the mountains above Idaho Springs, I found myself looking off in the direction of the resort. There, between two clusters of snowcapped peaks, I noticed a curious arched light, a ray pure and serene. Right then and there, I knew why the Indians had named Idaho Springs the Gem of the Mountains.

Dunton Hot Springs

Dolores County

Dunton Hot Springs
Dunton Route
Dolores, Colorado 81323
(No phone)

Location: Thirteen miles northwest of the town of Dolores on Route 145, then twenty-two miles on West Dolores Road (a primitive, gravel, national forest access road)
Elevation: 8,800 feet
Temperature: 107°F (42°C)
Flow: 20 gallons per minute
Services: Status uncertain. Inquire locally.

I drove into the town of Dolores and stopped at the ranger station to pick up a topographical map and to get some updated information on Dunton Hot Springs. What I learned was disappointing, to say the least. The hot spring and the town had been closed to the public since the last time I visited the area, ten years ago. The town now stood empty, a relic of the past. The ranger explained that unsafe drinking water was the reason for the closure. He told me I could still visit Dunton, but a soak in the springs was definitely out of the question.

It takes a traveler with a rustic eye to appreciate a place like Dunton Hot Springs, a crumbling shantytown surrounded by the rugged San Juan National Forest. This historic mining town was built in the late 1800s by Horatio Dunton. On my last visit, the town consisted of a bar, restaurant, dance hall, bathhouse, and a few cabins, all built in the nineteenth century, and all heated by potbellied wood-burning stoves.

But today you can't even get a glass of water in Dunton, and it's sad because the little hot-spring town holds more than a hundred years of history in its old cabins. Nobody seems to know the fate of Dunton. I hope someone will have the good sense to preserve it for future generations. Until then, the national forest surrounding the springs still offers some of the best elk hunting in the world and will always be one of Colorado's most popular recreation areas.

Paradise Hot Springs

Dolores County

Location: Just off State Highway 145. Ten miles north of the town of Rico and 2.6 miles south of Dunton on the northeast bank of the West Dolores River; 2.5 miles west of Eagle Peak
Elevation: 9,000 feet
Temperature: 115°F (46°C)
Flow: 26 to 34 gallons per minute
Services: Not open to the public

Once upon a time, the sodium springs here poured their hot water into a large outdoor swimming pool. Successive waves of pleasure seekers wandered through the area in a quest for health but seldom settled in it for long. Today the large pool is empty, and a rustic cabin built over one of the springs is all that remains of the glory days. Visitors are not welcome here anymore. The owner has had his property abused one too many times, and according to one report, he meets trespassers with a shotgun loaded with rock salt. So much for "once upon a time."

Manitou Springs

El Paso County

Location: I-25 south to Colorado Springs. Take U.S. 24 exit, then go five miles west of Colorado Springs.
Elevation: 6,336 feet
Temperature: Cold springs

Manitou Springs, once a famous spa and pleasure resort at the foot of Pikes Peak, is a city that hasn't lost its heritage. Twenty-four mineral springs are preserved in the city, but only one—Manitou Spring—had a spa and facilities for a hot mineral bath. However, its bathhouse closed in 1990. Today the building is home to a number of small shops.

Most of Manitou's springs are cold and issue from romantic fountains throughout the city. You are invited to drink the magic nectar from these springs, which many picnickers have called "lemonade springs" because of the luscious drink they make from the water. According to early records, the carbonated waters were once bottled and shipped statewide to drugstore soda fountains. Old-timers say you've never tasted a real ice cream soda until you've tasted one made with Manitou soda water.

In 1881, the railroad advertised Manitou Springs as "the most romantic and renowned watering place of the Rocky Mountains and the tourist center of Colorado." Many people would say that Manitou Springs is a "tourist trap," but nobody can deny that this is one of the most romantic spots in the world. History and beauty are everywhere.

One of Colorado's first and finest hotels, the Cliff House, is located on a quiet tree-lined street behind the Manitou Spa. This gingerbread

Woodland Park
24
To Hartsel
Green Mt. Falls
24
To Denver
25
Manitou Springs
Pikes Peak 14,110 ft.
Gold Camp Rd.
24
To Limon
Colorado Springs
Phanton Canyon
115
Manitou Springs
Canon City
50
Campgrounds
Major highway
Divided highway
N
Pueblo Reservoir
Pueblo
50
25
To Walsenburg

Victorian-style hostelry was built in 1874, and it was expanded to two hundred rooms in 1880, with a grab bag of balconies, turrets, and cupolas, and a broad veranda on which its guests sat in wicker rocking chairs and watched the world go by. In the basement of the building was a tunnel that led to the baths and Soda Spring. The Spa was so popular that it attracted visitors from all over the country: Theodore Roosevelt, Thomas Edison, and Lillian Russell among them.

Today the Cliff House is empty because it was damaged badly by a fire in 1982. There is talk of converting it into an apartment building; and some even want the old building razed, which would surely inspire a shock wave of sadness and nostalgia as another chapter of western history is closed to the public forever. I doubt if the resort was constructed to last centuries, but if it is preserved, people may look at it a hundred years from now and see that there were people with foresight once upon a time in Colorado, or at least in Manitou Springs.

In 1976, a reporter with the *Colorado Springs Sun* revealed the legend of Manitou Springs: "As the story goes, an old retired Indian Chief, looking for a quiet place to die, accidentally stumbled into the soda springs at the foot of Pikes Peak. He came out sopping wet, but he was a young man again." This is a cute story, but it doesn't do justice to the original Ute tale, which is full of majesty and mystery.

According to the Ute creation legend, the Manitou was the only god in heaven, and he lived all alone in the center of the sky, ruling the sun and the rain and the snow. But the Manitou was lonely and he wished for new work to do. So he bored a big hole in the floor of heaven, which is the sky, and when he looked through the hole he saw the nothingness beyond. He poured the rain and the snow through the big hole, then he gathered up all the dirt and the stones from the floor of heaven and poured this through the hole in the sky also. After he had poured for days, he looked through the hole at the world he had created. Below him he saw a great mountain (Pikes Peak) and a vast barren plain all covered with snow. The Manitou wished for something to make this world more beautiful, so he crawled through the hole in the sky and stepped down on the earth he had created. He stopped to touch the bare rock with his fingers, and wherever he touched, trees, flowers, grass, and forests sprang forth. Then the sun shone through the hole in the sky and melted the snow. Streams of water ran down the mountain and formed great lakes. Rivers flowed and the seas grew. Everything grew, and the world became very beautiful. The Manitou was so pleased that from that day on, after his work in the heavens was done, he came down from his home in the sky to roam the forests and the fields. His favorite spot was by the side of the springs.[1]

These are the names of the springs: Big Indian, Little Chief, Ouray, Ute, Geyser, Twin, Strantton, Navajo Geyser, 7-minute, Mansion 1, Mansion 2, Shoshone, Nishatunga, Sequoia, Manitou, Navajo, Cheyenne, Wheeler, Hiawatha, Magnetic, Little, Geyser Valve, Ute Chief, and Gusher.

Notes

1. Helen Sloan Daniels, "Ute Creation Legend," in *The Ute Indians of Southwestern Colorado* (Durango, Colo.: Public Library, 1941).

Canon City Hot Spring

Fremont County

Location: In the valley of the Arkansas River, at the southwest end of Riverside Drive in Canon City, a few miles from the eastern end of the Royal Gorge. Posted no hunting, no fishing. Private property.
Elevation: 8,000 feet
Temperature: 104°F (40°C)
Flow: Canon City Hot Spring has a discharge of about 5 gallons per minute. Nearby Soda Springs has a discharge so low that it has had the water pumped from it since as far back as 1920.
Services: Not for public use

The site of Canon City Hot Spring, at the lower end of the Royal Gorge, was used by the Utes long before the coming of the white men. Zebulon Pike discovered these springs when he entered the canyon in 1806. Although he returned here in 1807 to celebrate his twenty-eighth birthday, these springs didn't attract much attention until around 1901, when a railroad was built to connect Cripple Creek, Florence, and Canon City.

By 1877, the impact that these springs might have on the area was realized. This was the year Helen Hunt Jackson wrote: "No doubt, in a few years Canon City will largely be known as a resort for invalids, for the winter climate is a very pleasant one, much milder and warmer than that of Colorado Springs, and, therefore, better for many consumptives. Moreover, there are bubbling up in the limestone rocks at the mouth of the Grand Canyon; several nauseous hot springs, variously medicated and the class of people who will drink this water is a large and nomadic one." And in 1883, the *Canon City Record* wrote, "What is there to see in Canon City?" The answer was: "Soda Springs, Iron Springs and the hot soda baths."

Canon City eventually went on to become a popular resort area. A quote from a newspaper article dated 1894 read: "This is the recipient of many a 'lunger' sent here to die or be cured by the high dry climate . . . Spas, such as Soda Springs located one mile west of Canon City, are plentiful throughout the state and patronized for their curative powers."

The most famous of all Canon City's spas was the Royal Gorge Hotel. Situated on the south shore of the Arkansas River, this classy thirty-eight-room resort was built in the 1870s. It was a popular stomping ground of the miners from Leadville. When mining declined around the turn of the century, so did business at the hotel. It never quite recovered its former glory and "years later joined most of its ilk as a victim of the wrecker's ball."[1]

Although all of the springs are inaccessible to the public, there are other amusements that are worthwhile to the traveler. A trip to Phantom Canyon is always a delight. Just west of town you won't want to miss the renowned Royal Gorge Bridge (The world's highest suspension bridge. There is a toll.). This is also the site of the world's steepest incline railway, along with an aerial tramway, miniature railway, picnic areas, trails, narrow-gauge display, and Cliff Terrace Cafe. The best scenic drive in Canon City is up Skyline Drive, a long, fingerlike mesa that protrudes like a peninsula high above the town (great for night photos), and down the red hogback mountain behind the state penitentiary. Today Soda Springs is overshadowed by this forbidding building. The spa has disappeared, and what remains of the once-beloved Canon City Hot Spring is an abandoned swimming pool surrounded by a heap of twisted weeds, an unhonored and forgotten relic of a time that is past and gone.

Notes

1. Sandra Dallas, *No More than Five in a Bed* (Norman: University of Oklahoma Press, 1967), pp. 151-153.

Florence Artesian Well

Fremont County

Location: One-half mile west of the intersection of U.S. 50 and Route 115, east of the town of Florence
Elevation: 5,186 feet
Temperature: 81°F (27°C)
Flow: 130 gallons per minute
Services: Not for public use

Just a few years ago this was the site of the Hygienic Plunge Swimming Pool. Measuring 50 by 150 feet, the pool was one of the largest in the state. The highly mineralized water, aerated with carbon dioxide gas, was discovered in 1899, but it wasn't developed as a spa until the early 1920s. When the American Nauheim Baths were built, health seekers around the nation flocked to the area. This became one of the state's top spas, and hundreds testified to the benefits of the soothing baths. The medicinal water was also used for drinking.

After the Colorado School of Mines analyzed the water, the spa was advertised "as second to none in the United States and equaled by only one other in the world—the Bad Nauheim Spa in Germany."

Now, this is the site of a sewage treatment plant. Another hot plunge bites the dust, falling prey to the shifting tastes of the American public and the pressures of the population explosion. Does this mean that hot springs are really on the road to extinction?

It means another serious blow to Colorado's cultural heritage and, worse, it means that we can no longer lounge at the American Nauheim Baths and tell our friends that we have visited the only spa in the world that is equal to the Bad Nauheim Spa in Germany.

Fremont Natatorium Well

Fremont County

Location: Located in the northeast corner of Canon City
Elevation: 5,100 feet
Temperature: 96.8°F (36°C)
Flow: 125 to 150 gallons per minute
Services: Not for public use

The Fremont Natatorium ("natatorium" comes from the alternative name for sodium and natrium) was once supplied with mineral water by a 1,655-foot thermal well. The swimming pool is no longer in use.

According to the Colorado Geological Survey, the heating of the waters is probably caused by the decay of radioactive minerals, and the extreme depth of the well suggests that the water comes from the principal aquifer in the Canon City area—the Dakota Formation.

Wellsville Warm Spring

Fremont County

Location: Just off U.S. 50, approximately six miles southwest of Salida on the north bank of the Arkansas River
Elevation: 6,995 feet
Temperature: 82° to 91°F (28° to 33°C)
Services: Not for public use

The little town of Wellsville is just 5.2 miles east of Salida. There are no stores or services here—only a few scattered ranch homes and trailers. If you're looking for a place to swim, forget it! But if you're in the market to buy some tropical freshwater fish, come on down and have a look around.

A wooden bridge will take you across the Arkansas River and onto a dirt road that runs east past a large mill. Just before you reach the railroad tracks, make a right turn onto a private road that winds down to the springs. Here you'll see a cluster of dilapidated shacks that have given up fighting off decay. The sagging gray buildings are extremely weathered; the dry wood hasn't seen paint in years. The ancient concrete pools are chipped and broken, almost reverting back to a natural state. Still, Ed Finch and his brother-in-law have raised fish and tropical plants commercially in the warm waters since 1966. Nothing fancy, mind you (the selection seems rather limited). It's mostly a hobby these days, and many of the customers are small merchants from communities surrounding Wellsville.

Wellsville was first developed as a spa in 1915 (when the original concrete pools were built), but its heyday was back in the 1940s. Busloads of city folk would come up from Denver just to spend the day at this classy watering hole. Time has changed all that.

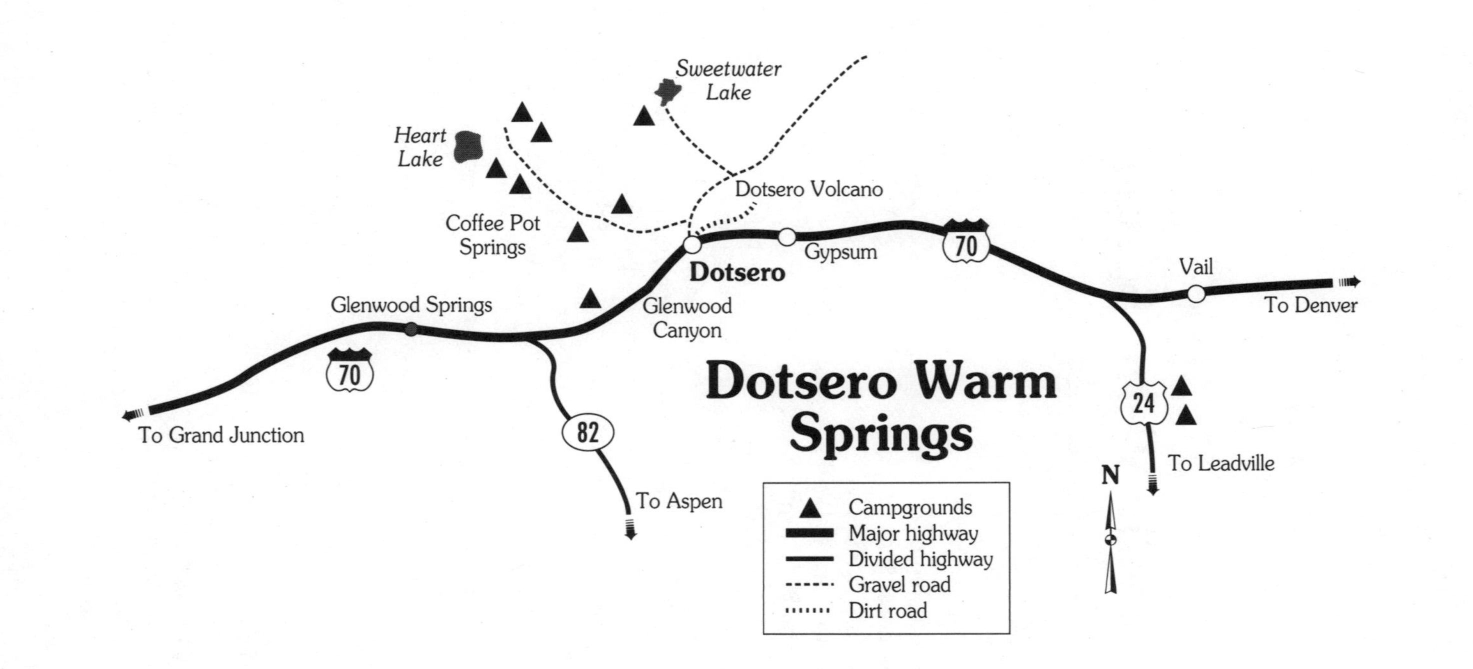
Sweetwater Lake
Heart Lake
Dotsero Volcano
Coffee Pot Springs
Dotsero
Gypsum
70
Vail
To Denver
Glenwood Springs
Glenwood Canyon
70
To Grand Junction
82
To Aspen
Dotsero Warm Springs
24
To Leadville
N
Campgrounds
Major highway
Divided highway
Gravel road
Dirt road

Dotsero Warm Springs

Garfield County

Location: Four miles west of Dotsero and approximately one-half mile upstream from the entrance of Glenwood Canyon
Elevation: 5,600 feet
Temperature: 90°F (32°C)
Flow: Approximately 1,800 to 2,000 gallons per minute
Services: None

The town of Dotsero consists of the Dotsero Block Company and a cluster of small houses and trailers. It is located east of Glenwood Springs on I-70, and you're apt to drive past the unassuming little town without even knowing it. I had on many occasions. The first few times I visited Dotsero I camped up near Coffee Pot Springs and Deep Lake. I spent most of my time scouting the west bank of the Colorado River for hot springs. In 1980 I met a crew of county surveyors who were surveying the land for the highway department. I asked if they knew where the hot springs were located, but they weren't exactly sure. Later, I asked a state geologist, who told me to visit during the winter; with the steam rising, it's easy to pinpoint hot springs. That information wasn't much use to me. In 1982 the highway department expanded I-70 to a four-lane freeway and plowed over the old bathhouse spring and some of the bigger springs in the area. On the east bank of the river, however, there are many untouched hot springs. These springs are best known and most accessible to the boatmen who float this stretch of the river.

I thought that the best way to find out about other hot springs in Dotsero would be to drive into town and ask someone. When I drove up, Ronald Tobiason (known as Toby to everyone in town) was in his driveway, loading up his '68 Ford station wagon with tools. A man in his mid-fifties, Toby was a friendly sort of guy who was willing to share what he knew about Dotsero.

The next thing I knew, Toby was introducing me to his neighbors, Frank and Ileen Daley. Ileen was born in Dotsero and has lived most of her life here. Her heritage stems from a long line of railroaders. As a matter of fact, her house was once the old railroad depot; it even served a stint as the post office.

Soon we were all sitting around the kitchen table, drinking coffee and eating moist apple cake with buttercream frosting. Ileen told me how Dotsero had once been a hub of activity. The trains stopped there every day. From Dotsero, the trains either cut down south toward Leadville or continued straight on through to Glenwood Springs and then on to Salt Lake City, Utah. In the early 1900s, this was known as the Dotsero Cutoff. Not only did the trains drop off the mail, but they also dropped off groceries from the nearby town of Glenwood. Dotsero was once quite a little town; it supported two saloons and a grocery store, but that was a long time ago.

Today, nothing much happens in Dotsero. The talk of the day was about the mountain lion that was terrorizing the sheep. It had already killed a dog, and still nobody in town had taken out a permit to shoot the cat. We also talked about the springs and the thermal caves along the banks of the Colorado River. The book *Caves of Colorado* reports numerous caverns (Groaning Cave and Fixin' to Die Cave) around Coffee Pot Springs and Dotsero. Toby warned me about the dangers of these caves and cliffs. Apparently, the fragile limestone cliffs break away quite easily. Not only that, but if you go sticking your face in enough cracks and crevices, you just might be surprised by a wildcat or skunk.

After we finished eating the cake, Toby invited me to accompany him and his wife to the top of the volcano. Since nobody visits Dotsero anymore, I guess I was somewhat of an oddity. I accepted.

Although this land is in the public domain, the Dotsero Block Company has exclusive rights to the road leading up to the volcano. After all, they built the road in order to mine cinder for their blocks. On the way up we had to stop. Three earth-moving machines and a couple of dump trucks blocked the way. Toby got out and told one of the workmen that we were going to the top of the volcano to get some diamonds. The man said that we didn't have to go all the way to the top for diamonds, that we could find them right here. He said that he sees them every day.

Finally, one of the dump trucks pulled to the side, and we drove under a conveyor belt that was hauling and dumping the volcanic ash into a gigantic sifter. The ash sparkled with diamonds as it splashed on the hood of the car.

At the edge of the rim, we looked into the gaping crater. Toby told me that the last time he was up here he could see a backpacker down in the crater. Toby also told me that he once considered hunting deer down there, but he said that he wouldn't do it if he wasn't planning on cooking and eating it down there, because he sure as hell wasn't going to pack it out of that crater. We looked for the mountain lion, but all we found, as Toby promised, was a fistful of Dotsero diamonds (about 8.5 on the hardness scale).

Although the bathhouse is gone, I still had a good feeling while I was visiting Dotsero. If I had had more time, perhaps I would have checked out some of the old homesteads. The trout fishing along this stretch of the Colorado is also supposed to be excellent. Someday I might even drive two miles west into White River National Forest and invest twelve dollars for a day of white-water rafting.

East of Dotsero Springs (at the confluence of the Colorado River and the Eagle River) is Dotsero Saline Springs. This particular group of springs, along with Glenwood Saline Springs (a few miles west of Glenwood, where the Colorado River and the Roaring Fork River divide), has environmentalists concerned. These springs are loading the Colorado River and its tributaries with salt and are damaging the water. Some 5 million tons of salt are deposited into the river each year, causing $23 million in damages annually. The Bureau of Reclamation has determined that these hot springs are one of the largest points of pollution to the Colorado River, and since the United States shares the water with Mexico, the Department of the Interior has set new requirements for cleaning up the river. Today environmentalists are exploring an acceptable, efficient way to reduce the salt entering the Colorado River so that it will remain safe for years to come.

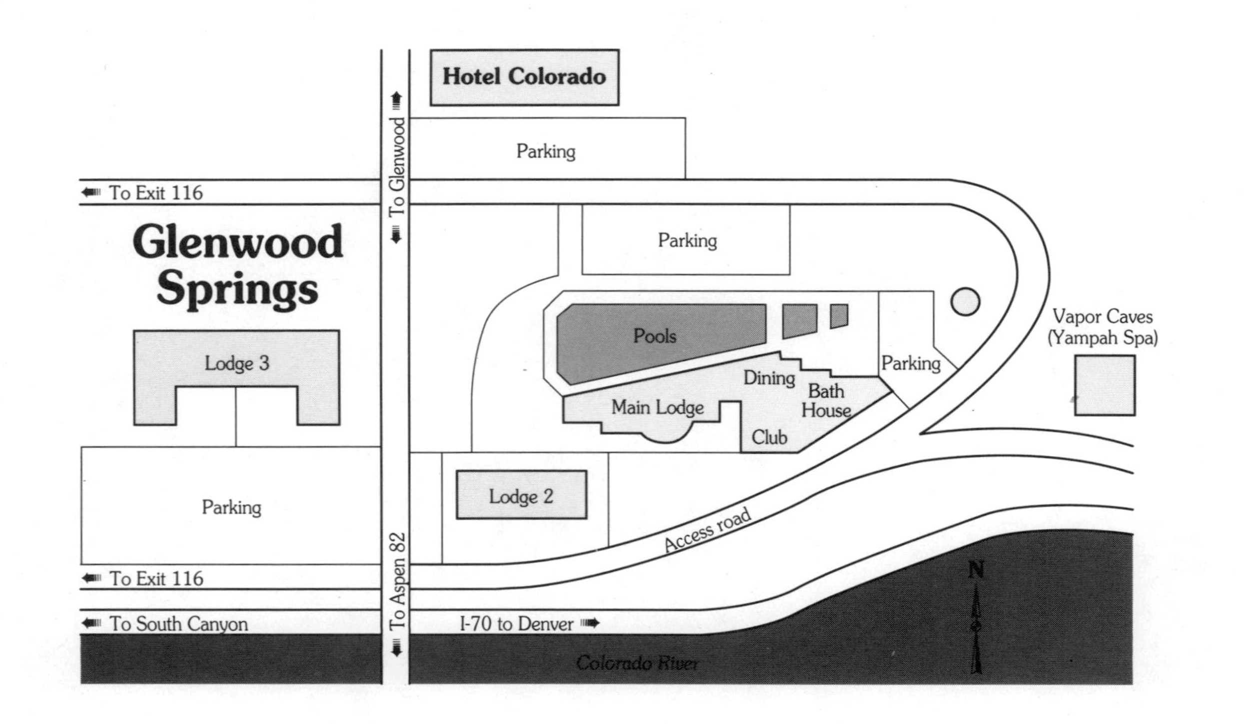
Glenwood Springs
Hotel Colorado
Parking
To Glenwood
To Exit 116
Parking
Pools
Lodge 3
Parking
Dining
Bath House
Main Lodge
Club
Vapor Caves (Yampah Spa)
Parking
Lodge 2
Access road
To Exit 116
To Aspen 82
To South Canyon
I-70 to Denver
Colorado River
N

Glenwood Springs

Garfield County

Glenwood Springs Hot Springs Lodge
Box 308
Glenwood Springs, Colorado 81602
(303) 945-6571 or 1-800-537-7946

Location: One block off Interstate 70 at exit 116
Elevation: 5,800 feet
Temperature: 111° to 124°F (44° to 51°C)
Flow: 3,000 gallons per minute combined flow of all springs
Services: All major credit cards accepted. One hundred and seven rooms, cable TV, restaurant, gift shop, health club, ten-speed bicycle rental, wading pool, and large pool with jet chairs on premises. The city of Glenwood is just one block away. Open all year.

It is commonly accepted as historical fact that Glenwood Springs around the turn of the century possessed a certain graciousness and feeling for the good things in life. Although a new generation inhabits the magnificent resort and grand hotel these days, some would say that the feeling has hardly changed.

With about three thousand swimmers visiting the pool each summer day, the Glenwood Lodge is hardly a place to get away from it all. Still, it's worth a visit. Today the town is filled with bonanza real estate kings, Aspen ski bums, and harried young businessmen on vacation. The desk clerks at both the Hotel Colorado and the Glenwood Lodge admit that the rich and famous still come to Glenwood Springs for a good time, just as they did in the old days: John Denver swims in the pool from time to time, and sun-loving George Hamilton has been seen lounging around the side of the pool (if you're a sun worshipper set on a total tan, Glenwood is the perfect place to be.

Glenwood Springs is the granddaddy of all the hot-spring resorts in Colorado. In 1890, the passenger department of the Rock Island and Pacific Railway published a guidebook that claimed Glenwood Springs was "the chosen Mecca for visitors of ample means and leisure." That statement is as true today as it was yesterday: In the early days, some of the nation's greatest men walked the streets of Glenwood. Some of the notables—famous and infamous—that came to whoop it up at the hotel and resort included Diamond Jim Brady, the Mayo Brothers, Buffalo Bill Cody, and Doc Holliday. But in 1905 a visitor arrived that gave Glenwood an elite mark of distinction that would set it apart from the other towns as someplace special, as one of the nation's greatest resorts. That visitor was President Theodore Roosevelt, who came to town on a three-week bear hunt. In 1909 Glenwood was visited by another president, William Howard Taft.

Today the town remains much the same as it did in the early days. The great 500-foot-long swimming pool, which was built in 1888, is still in use today. The old train depot is still located across the river from the charming Hotel Colorado. And the Rio Grande Railway still brings visitors to the town three times a week (reservations are recommended). The passenger train leaves Denver early in the morning and takes you through some of the most breathtaking scenery in the world on its way to Salt Lake City, but of course you're not going that far. You're going to Glenwood, which is just around the next bend. Off in the distance, surrounded by a cloud of purple haze, you see the historic resort. The hot steam rising around the building gives the grand old resort a spooky dignity. When the train stops at the Art Deco train depot, you'll get your first good look at Glenwood the Magnificent.

Sure, things have changed a little since the 1800s. The newly installed turbo-tube—a winding tubular slide—and the miniature golf course weren't here in the old days, but then again, neither were the Olympic diving board, the health club, nor all the fine skiing areas that are within easy driving distance: Aspen, Snowmass, Sunlight, and Vail.

But for those who like to hike, fish, camp, and climb rocks, the scenic wonders of the area are still splendid and unspoiled. The Colorado River and its tributaries, although a little more sluggish than in the old days, offer some of the best fishing in the state, and the numerous canyons—No

Name Canyon, Grizzly Canyon, Dead Horse Canyon, Glenwood Canyon, and 11-mile Canyon—have some wild and awe-inspiring rock formations that would be a challenge to any climber. In the winter, ice climbers might want to test their skills out on Hidden Falls or Glenwood Falls. There is also a hiking trail two miles above the mouth of Dead Horse Canyon that winds through the whispering pines along a clear sparkling creek and eventually leads you to one of the most beautiful waterfalls in the Rocky Mountains—Bridal Falls.

If it wasn't for one of Colorado's early dream weavers—Captain Issac Cooper, an ailing Leadville miner and Civil War veteran who purchased the springs in 1882 and promoted the town, naming it after his native Glenwood, Iowa—the town might not be what it is today. Cooper envisioned a European-style spa along the banks of the river, but his miner friends thought that he was following his dreams to the point of folly, if not madness. No one was interested in a town with no silver or gold.

At first the people who came here copied the Indian method of bathing by scooping holes in the ground under the shady pines. Eventually, a crude bathhouse was built. But it wasn't until 1885 that things really began to change; this was the year the Colorado Midland Railroad announced its plans to build a standard-gauge railroad from Colorado Springs to Aspen. The rich ore of the Aspen silver mines was the sought-after prize.

Glenwood grew. The sound of saws and hammers at work echoed in the streets. Huge wagons thundered over the mountains to bring back red sandstone bricks from Canyon Diablo. The dark red hue of the canyon bricks gave the town a handsome and elegant character. At dusk the romantic streets were illuminated by incandescent electric lights. By 1890 the lodge, known as the Bath House, was completed; its construction changed the course of the river and cost the town more than $100,000. In 1891 the Hotel Colorado, a copy of the Villa Medici in Rome, was under construction; by the time it was completed, it had an estimated value of $850,000. In five years the small town of 200 people grew into a mountain city of 2,500 residents.

Cooper died before he could see his dream come to life, but Chief Colorow, whose tribe was driven to a dusty reservation in Utah when the first white settlers arrived, returned to Glenwood many times to see the white man's progress. Later in his life he wandered the streets, a lonely and broken man, nothing more than a common beggar. A touching story has been told that explains Colorow's sorry condition:

When Colorow was a young boy, his tribe adopted a beautiful white child they found wandering, lost and alone, on a mountain trail. The tribe named her Spirit. When she was sixteen, she married Colorow, and they lived happily until the day Spirit became ill. Colorow took her to the Yampah (Big Medicine) Spring. A few days later the white girl was well again. But on the journey home, she was thrown from her horse and died a few hours later. It is said that Colorow, when he was an old man, sometimes stood on the brink of the Yampah and watched the steam rising in the swimming pool, a steam that sometimes appeared in the form of his beloved Spirit.[1]

Anyone with even a passing familiarity with the history of the West will be impressed with the town's rich cultural heritage, with all the tall tales and legends that seem to go on forever. Glenwood has many engrossing faces and facets, and all it takes is a walk through the streets, lined with historic houses and buildings, to discover the real charm of the little city. Many of the old saloons are still standing, and they serve the same libations they did in the early days. You can also find Doc Holliday's gravestone in the cemetery.

The only problem is that it sometimes seems that every other living human on the planet has discovered Glenwood's magnificent resort. It's not surprising, since Glenwood has something for everybody: Here you can enjoy a swim in a hot mineral water pool surrounded by glistening snow-crowned peaks—any season of the year, whether August or December—rafting, rock climbing, and horseback riding. And if you don't do any of those things, it might be kind of fun to be under the same roof that covered Teddy Roosevelt and Doc Holliday.

Notes

1. Frances Melrose, "Hotel of a Thousand Stories," *Rocky Mountain News*, 29 December 1946.

Glenwood Springs Vapor Caves

Garfield County

Yampah Spa
709 East 6th Street
Glenwood Springs, Colorado 81601
(303) 945-0667

Location: One block off Interstate 70 at exit 116, just east of the Hot Spring Lodge and Pool
Elevation: 5,800 feet
Temperature: 122°F (50°C)
Flow: 5 gallons per minute
Services: Vapor baths, massages, facials, herbal body mud treatments. Robes, towels, and locker provided. Open seven days a week from 9:00 A.M. to 9:00 P.M.

(See map on page 62.)

At the mouth of Glenwood Canyon, just a few hundred feet across the parking lot from the lodge pool, is a separate building that houses the Vapor Caves. Upstairs, a full course of therapeutic activities is offered for the modern health seeker. Downstairs, every known type of bath is given except the old Indian ceremonial bath in which it was fashionable to wrap oneself in the freshly removed hide of a grizzly bear.

As you descend the twenty sandstone steps toward the entrance to the caves, you begin to feel the steamy, stifling heat. The strong sulphur dioxide gas, which is released by the spring, has a suffocating effect at first. Your breathing becomes heavy, and beads of sweat begin to trickle down your forehead into your eyes. You are about to experience one of Mother Nature's most delightful wonders: a natural steam bath.

Ahead, the penetrating half-light reveals huge marble slab benches surrounding the spring. These benches, now yellowed with age, were installed back in 1893, at the same time the cave house was wired with electricity. This was an era of great accomplishment: The Victorian resort, the acre-sized pool, and the grand Hotel Colorado had all been built within a few years. But the raging productivity of the Victorians shattered nerves. More than ever, people needed a place to relax and recuperate, and the vapor cave was the best place to sweat out the evils of a hyperactive life. In those days of prudery, bathing attire consisted of huge muslin bags, hardly suitable for a 120-degree steam bath. Today the atmosphere is more casual.

There are three natural caves here: two small caves for men and one large cave for women. Inside the misty chambers, you would almost expect to discover ancient Indian cave drawings and inscriptions, but the Utes who were the first to use the caves didn't come to paint graffiti on the walls with delicate animal-hair brushes. The Utes came because the *Yampah* (Big Medicine) bubbled up through the floor in the cavern.

This cave was of immense importance to the Utes, as it is to all the people who come here today seeking relief from arthritis, asthma, sinus problems, nervous strain, colds, and kidney disease, as well as a host of other disorders. The Utes entered the cavern by crawling through a large hole in the ceiling. Although this hole has long since been sealed off, you'll still find evidence of the entryway in the women's cave. In the Ute view of the universe this was a holy site, and the Indians made annual spring pilgrimages to the springs to partake in religious bathing rites.

After the long, bitter Colorado winters, the soothing waters brought new life to the body and the spirit. It's easy to imagine a weary warrior finding sanctuary in this cave: He sits on his haunches as a shaft of light beams through the roof, spotlighting the spring. He watches the hot steam rise like spirits toward the blue sky. This is the stuff that mystical experiences are made of. This was big medicine. It seems strange that the Utes would also use these caves as a form of punishment, but they did. Impudent braves were sometimes sealed in the dark, hot recesses of the mountain until they were willing to conform to tribal customs.

In a roundabout way, the Utes were the first to advertise the hidden springs to the rest of the world. In 1879, stories of a miraculous spring whispered through the pines down the mountain to Leadville. This is where Isaac Cooper, the founder of Glenwood, first heard of the vapor cave, which the Indians praised for its tremendous healing powers. At this time Cooper was still a young man, but he had grown old and weary before his time; the Civil War had left him worse from wear and tear, and ever since then he had been living the depraved life of a Leadville miner. His health was fading.

Cooper and a few of his prospector friends set out on an expedition in the dead of winter. They snowshoed sixty miles over the Continental Divide, and when they eventually reached the spring, Cooper knew that this was where he would live the rest of his life. Here he would build a town that emphasized health rather than wickedness.

Although health is still emphasized at the Vapor Caves, don't expect to find a multimillion-dollar mecca with juice bar, quadraphonic stereo, and babysitting services. There are no fancy frills here—just a clean, professional atmosphere. The masseurs and masseuses are well trained, the equipment is in good condition, and the specialty of the house is ultimate relaxation.

So if you're feeling crowded by the world with all its tensions and obligations, escape to the Vapor Caves and let the thermal heat relax your body and quiet your mind. This is truly Big Medicine.

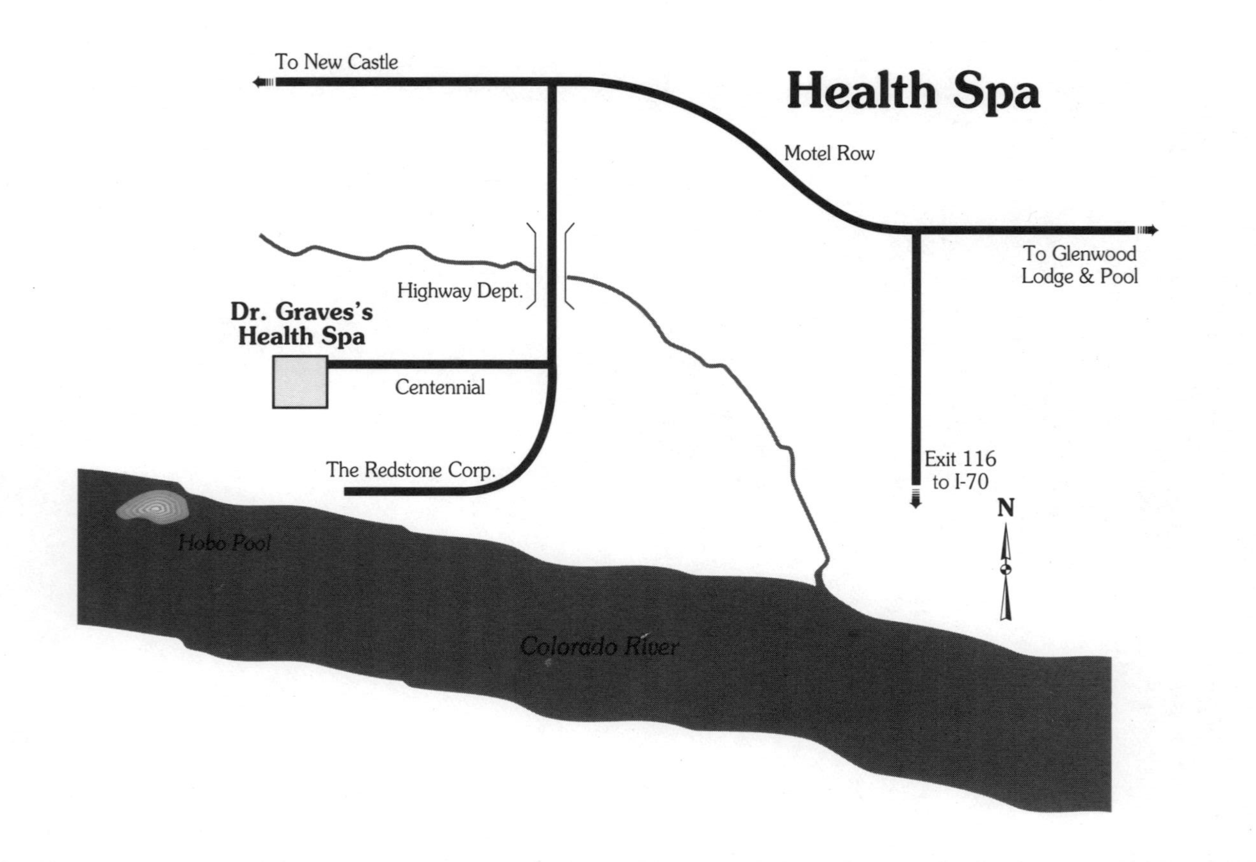

Health Spa
To New Castle
Motel Row
To Glenwood
Lodge & Pool
Highway Dept.
Dr. Graves's
Health Spa
Centennial
The Redstone Corp.
Exit 116
to I-70
N
Hobo Pool
Colorado River

Health Spa

Garfield County

Health Spa
0281 Centennial Road
Glenwood Springs, Colorado 81601

Location: From the city of Glenwood Springs, take U.S. 6 west to Devereux Road, then turn south and follow the road to Centennial and turn right
Services: Six private individual hot tubs. Status uncertain; inquire locally.

Developed by Robert Wore in 1896, this is what remains of the once-famous West Glenwood Health Spa. In the old days, the rich from Glenwood came in their horse-drawn surreys to visit the spa. Eventually a three-story mansion was built to accommodate the guests. The red brick building was a showplace, nestled in an orchard of peach and apple trees along the west bank of the Colorado River. In 1939 a tourist shuttle service was operating between the spa and Glenwood Springs. Mineral baths cost twenty-five cents and were served with a complimentary glass of ice-cold buttermilk. As late as 1955 the *Saturday Evening Post* described it as one of the "places to go" in Colorado.

From 1968 to 1991, a chiropractor by the name of Charles Graves ran the little spa. He kept the public bathhouse and also used it for his patients. The good doctor once owned the property, and he's still quite fond of the place. Ten years ago, when he told me the story of the Hobo Pool, his face lit up and his eyes twinkled: "In the nineteen-thirties, the Rio Grande used to turn the trains around back there." He pointed out toward the gravel parking lot. "The hobos would get off the train here, and they'd set up camp on the other side of the orchard. They built rock pools along the riverbank and ate fruit from the trees and tried to live like rich folks." He tells me that the pools are still there.

I cut through the ten-acre orchard. The trees were blooming, and hundreds of brightly colored finches, orioles, and waxwings swarmed in waves from tree to tree. They made a glorious sound. It was like walking through a fantastic bird sanctuary. Finally, I reached the infamous Hobo Pool. These primitive rock pools were built along the river directly under a concrete cistern that has "Private Property-No Trespassing" stenciled on it. Someone obviously didn't believe the words.

On the way back through the orchard, I noticed that the trees hadn't been pruned in years. The old spa had definitely gone downhill since its glory days. I tried to imagine this place as the eye of Glenwood's social hurricane. I thought about the exclusive Saturday night dances that were once held in the old mansion. I thought about how much fun it must have been to dance to the music of the first Wurlitzer in town. And I wondered if the rundown little spa would ever regain some of its past splendor.

Today, the Redstone Corporation owns the property, and it hasn't yet announced any plans for the old resort. The spa closed altogether in 1991, but it reopened again in 1992 with a fresh paint job. Hot tubs, mud baths, and massages were the house specialties, yet the future of the spa remains uncertain.

South Canyon Hot Springs

Garfield County

Location: Located one-half mile south of I-70 in South Canyon west of Glenwood Springs. Take the South Canyon exit, then go south one-half mile on an old dirt road. The springs cannot be seen from the road but can be reached by a foot trail just off the road.
Elevation: 6,200 feet
Temperature: 118°F (48°C)
Flow: 7 to 17 gallons per minute
Services: None. Status uncertain; inquire locally.

Five miles west of Glenwood Springs on I-70 is an old dirt road—South Canyon—that winds up into the mountains toward the dump. It is about one-half mile from the highway to the infamous South Canyon Hot Springs. During the day you'll see huge dump trucks grinding their way up to the South Canyon Landfill site and back. In the ravine alongside the road you'll find an assortment of shoddy odds and ends—threadbare sofas and chairs with their foam guts oozing out, rusty bedsprings, moth-eaten mattresses, porcelain sinks, an occasional dead cat, and a lot of old tires. Just before the turnoff to the dump, on the right side of the road, is a place to pull over. Here an old footpath, overgrown with weeds, will lead you through a scrubby wooded area across a shallow creek to the springs. It isn't much to look at, is it? Well, it wasn't always like this.

Back in the 1960s you were lucky if you could find a place to park around here. Cars, vans, and pickups filled with long-haired hippies clogged the road. The flower children came by the VW busload to do drugs and get back to nature. This was the Woodstock generation who,

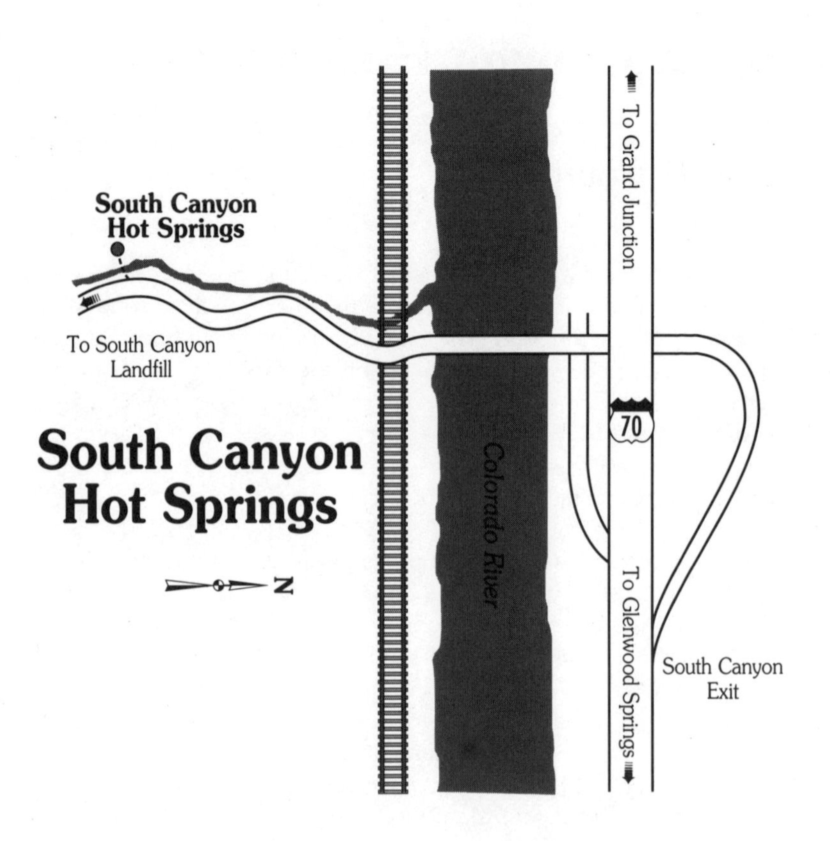

South Canyon
Hot Springs
To South Canyon
Landfill
South Canyon
Hot Springs
N
Colorado River
To Grand Junction
70
To Glenwood Springs
South Canyon
Exit

in the style of their day, believed in free love, peace, and exposing the hypocrisy of the establishment. They also believed in exposing themselves, especially in areas where Mother Nature provided unspoiled hot springs. Eventually, the hippies began to construct elaborate rock pools so that they could lie back in the deep purple water under the mellow yellow sun and listen to psychedelic music on their portable cassette tape players at full volume. South Canyon was a perfect place to forget the helter-skelter world of politics, big business, campus unrest, and if you could, the Vietnam War. For a while it was a hassle-free paradise.

Meanwhile, back in the town of Glenwood, the scene was altogether different. At the city council meetings, the South Canyon Springs was often a topic of heated debate: What were they going to do about the drug problem, the flagrant display of nudity, and the lack of sanitation up at the springs? Some were asking for a crackdown, because they believed that the longhairs were driving away tourists and tarnishing the image of Glenwood. Others were worried about the threat of social diseases that might spread through these roving gypsies, and still others wanted to exploit the springs and make a quick buck. But the town had no interest in commercially developing the springs, since it already had one of the finest hot spring resorts in the world. So they let it be, and eventually the springs became somewhat of a joke to the local residents; they called it "hippie dip."

Skinny-dipping continued to be popular throughout the 1970s, but in 1979 the city finally decided to render the springs useless by destroying them. It was mainly health concerns that caused the demise of the springs; the sanitation and drug problem had gotten way out of control.

At first it was rumored that the city had plans to bulldoze the area, but according to a freelance mason by the name of Bob, who rebuilt the pools in the summer of 1982, the city ruled against bulldozing the natural hot spring. Dynamite was also ruled out. Instead, the city workers came to the springs with their double-jack sledgehammers. The few spectators who watched the workers break away the carefully built cobblestone pools probably thought they were witnessing the life and death of a legend. But good legends die hard.

The two new cement-lined pools were eventually bulldozed, and with them a small piece of Colorado history was buried. But don't be surprised if you hear that these springs have surfaced again. History has a habit of repeating itself.

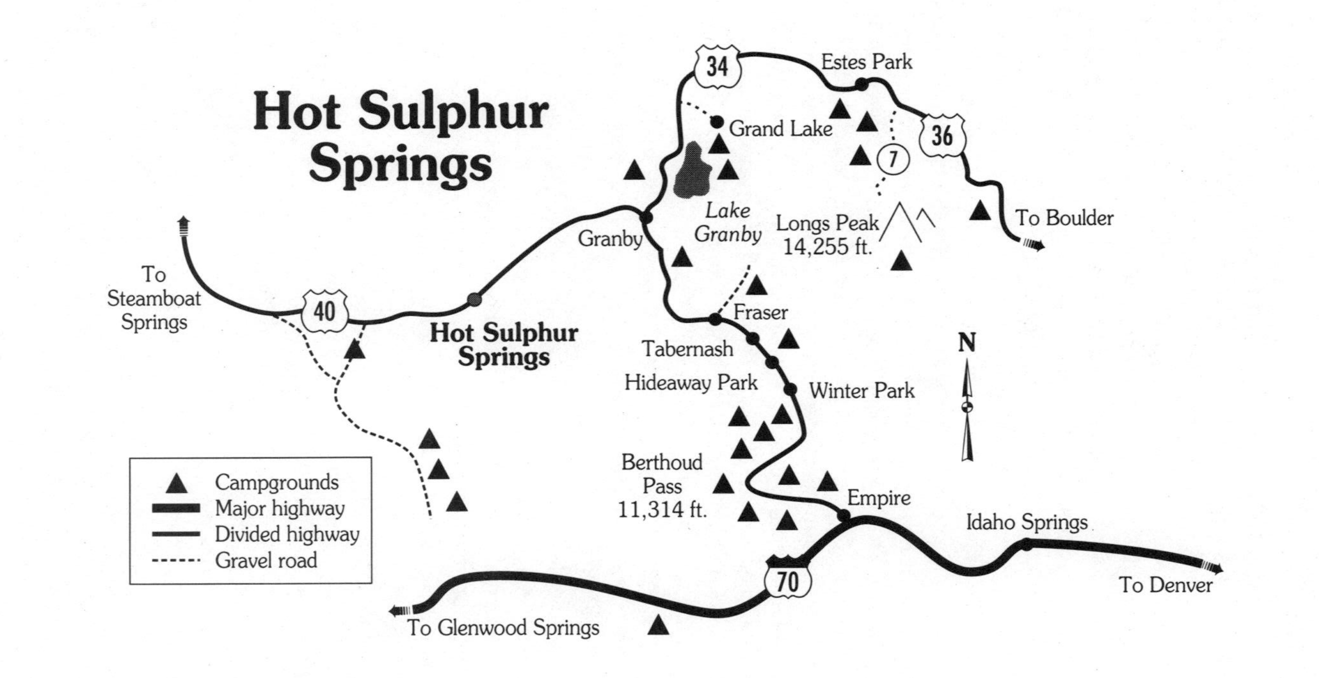
Hot Sulphur Springs
34
Estes Park
36
Grand Lake
7
Lake Granby
Longs Peak 14,255 ft.
To Boulder
Granby
To Steamboat Springs
40
Hot Sulphur Springs
Fraser
Tabernash
Hideaway Park
Winter Park
N
Berthoud Pass 11,314 ft.
Empire
Idaho Springs
70
To Denver
To Glenwood Springs
Campgrounds
Major highway
Divided highway
Gravel road

Hot Sulphur Springs

Grand County

Hot Sulphur Springs
Box 175
Hot Sulphur Springs, Colorado 80451
(303) 725-3306

Location: Just off U.S. 40 in the town of Hot Sulphur Springs. At the intersection of Park Street and Grand Avenue, follow the signs across the river to the resort.
Elevation: 7,625 feet
Temperature: 104° to 111°F (40° to 44°C)
Flow: 100 gallons per minute
Services: No credit cards. Rooms and camping spaces available. Open June through November.

For years, like the rest of Hot Sulphur Springs, this resort has been sinking into shabby senility. For a time it was one of the most successful spas in the state. The railroad actually drove a tunnel through the backbone of the Rockies just to reach Hot Sulphur Springs. But that was back in 1928 (and when the Moffat Tunnel was completed, it was the sixth longest tunnel in the Western Hemisphere, 6.1 miles in length). Today the Rio Grande Zephyr still flashes through the tunnel, but it no longer stops at Hot Sulphur Springs. The train emerges at Winter Park, and its first stop is at Granby (the closest you'll get to Hot Sulphur Springs). From here you can take the bus, which arrives in Hot Sulphur Springs twice a day.

Just a few blocks northwest of town, the resort is set in a bowl with mountains behind it and the Colorado River rushing alongside it (the trout fishing is splendid here). The Arapaho National Forest (1,009,000 acres) completely surrounds the quiet little town. Today this old resort provides an outdoor swimming pool, outdoor soaking pool, and four private sweat baths. But the old pool house stands like a phantom of the past.

People don't swim here anymore. The roof of the old building is collapsing, and the broken-down bleachers sit alongside the Olympic-sized pool, staring out at nothing.

There are as many as twenty to twenty-five springs in the area, all with a strong sulphurous odor. The channels through which the waters flow into the pools are lined with a soft yellowish substance that is velvety to the touch. The close similarity of the mineral content of the different springs allows the owner to combine the flow of all the springs into one for use in the pools and bathing house. The end result is the combined waters of the Big Spring, Bathhouse Spring, Combined Spring, Little Sulphur Spring, and Pool Spring.

According to Ute legend, the springs acquired curative powers in answer to an aging chief's prayers. Left by his tribe to die, the chief appealed to the Great Spirit and was granted magic powers. Under divine direction, he built an enchanted fire within the springs, and after bathing in the holy waters he recovered his health and rejoined his tribe.

Another version of the legend goes like this: Many years ago, long before the coming of the white man, an elderly chief led a group of young warriors to the springs. They camped, and the young braves talked through the night of crossing the Continental Divide to obtain scalps, horses, and plunder from the Plains Indians. But the wise old chief knew the foolishness of youth. He advised against the attack. Still, the young braves' hearts were touched with the fire of war, and the next morning they started on their journey over the mountains. The old chief waited for them. The day turned to night, and the mountain air turned cold. The chief built a fire in a gulch on Mount Bross (a 9,850-foot peak located directly behind the resort) and waited for the warriors to return. Many moons passed. And when the old man realized that the war was done and his young warriors were stone dead, he lay down by the springs and died. The old chief grieved himself to death, yet his campfire continued to burn, warming the springs and giving it healing properties.[1] From this time on, according to the Utes, any warriors that passed the

Hot Sulphur Springs in the 1920s. *(Courtesy Colorado Historical Society)*

springs would have a place to heal their wounds and ritualistically bathe their dead.

Hot Sulphur Springs was one of the greatest comforts of the Utes' many pilgrimages across the western United States. Even Chief Ouray once made a special trip to the springs in a quest for health. Suffering from a terrible attack of rheumatism, he had himself strapped to a buffalo skin stretcher between two horses, tandem fashion, and was transported from his home on the Uncompahgre to the springs. After bathing in the springs, the chief mounted his favorite pinto. The horse reared toward the sky, hooves boxing the sun; then they galloped back home together.[2]

This whole county is rich in Colorado history because it once belonged to the Utes. The relics of an era lived over a century ago can still be found here, and new archaeological discoveries are being made every day. The area known as Arapaho Pass was once the only practical place of entry to the county. The Utes built miles of stone wall and earthworks here to keep the Plains Indians from invading their territory.

A short distance from Hot Sulphur Springs, in the nearby town of Granby, ancient Ute forts have been found. According to Ute folklore and reports from leading Ute chiefs such as Douglas, Yarmony, and Washington, these forts were probably constructed in the early 1800s, about the same time that all the great Indian battles of Grand County were being fought. The fort near Granby was pretty well preserved until as late as 1939, when an arrowhead collector tore part of the fort down.[3]

Today the sleepy little town of Hot Sulphur Springs, with a population of about four hundred, is one of the most relaxing summer retreats in the state. Hunting and fishing are the most popular forms of recreation. In the winter you'll find snowmobiling and cross-country skiing at its best, and there are seven alpine ski areas, all within easy driving distance. And while we're on the subject of driving, one of the most incredible scenic drives in the world is just a short distance away. Just west of Granby, take U.S. 34 north past Lake Granby, Shadow Mountain Lake, and Grand Lake. Continue north and you'll reach Trail Ridge Road, which winds through Rocky Mountain National Park, climbing far above timberline into air so thin that looking at the mountains will literally take your breath away. At Estes Park, stop at the Stanley Hotel (restaurant, bar, and lodging). This colonial structure rises high above the little resort town, as magnificent as any hotel in Europe. If it sounds inviting, it is!

Notes

1. Wilson Rockwell, *The Utes—A Forgotten People* (Denver: Sage Books, 1956), pp. 19-20.
2. Rockwell, 22.
3. Rockwell, 19-20.

Cement Creek Warm Spring

Gunnison County

Cement Creek Ranch
Crested Butte, Colorado 81224
(303) 349-6512

Location: Twenty-one miles north of Gunnison and seven miles south of Crested Butte on Route 135, then follow signs to the ranch. Access is via a 4.5-mile dirt road running along Cement Creek.
Elevation: 9,500 feet
Temperature: Warm springs
Flow: 60 to 80 gallons per minute
Services: No credit cards. One rental cabin with kitchen. Fishing, hunting, hiking, miles of mountain bike trails, and horseback riding are available. Reservations for a minimum of one week are required. Open May to November.

Although Indians prowled this land more than a century ago (the Utes called it Cascadilla Creek), much of Cement Creek is still unexplored wilderness, and no hunters have yet hiked through much of the upland forest or set foot on alpine tundra. *Sports Illustrated* (February 19, 1979) said, "this is probably the best valley in the state for game," and as far as fishing goes, there are fifteen miles of trout streams and beaver ponds winding through the area. So it's easy to understand why the warm springs are sometimes overlooked.

Located at 9,000 feet, 250-acre Cement Creek Ranch is the highest private guest ranch in the United States, and it is surrounded by 1.7 million acres of the Gunnison National Forest. The ranch was homesteaded

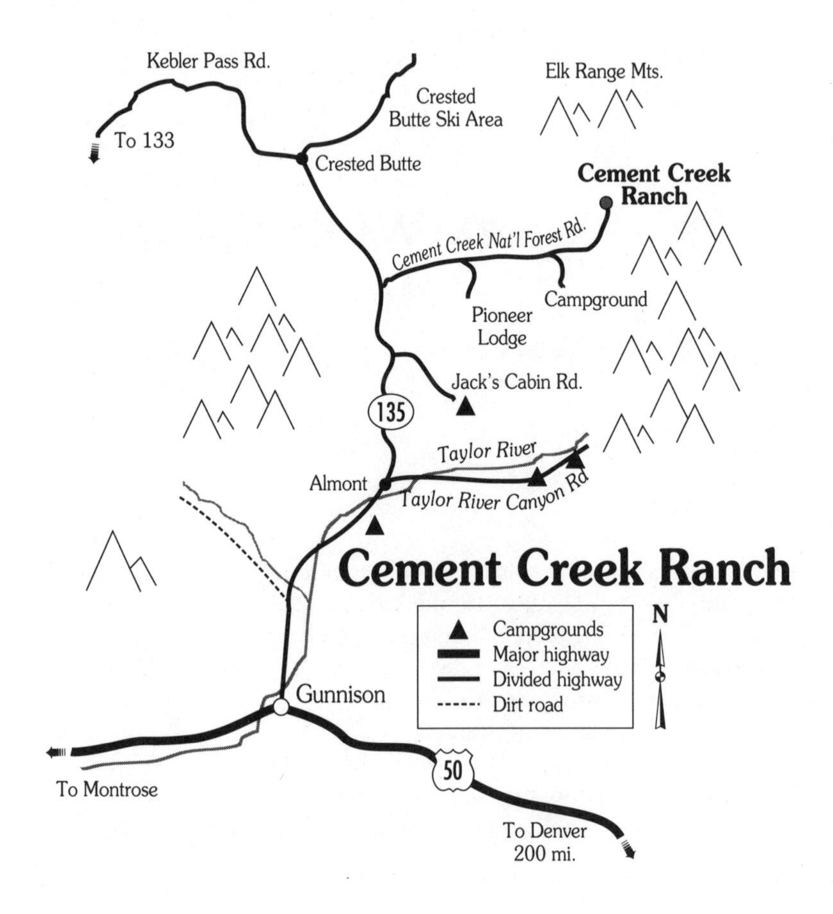

Kebler Pass Rd.
To 133
Crested Butte Ski Area
Crested Butte
Elk Range Mts.
Cement Creek Ranch
Cement Creek Nat'l Forest Rd.
Campground
Pioneer Lodge
Jack's Cabin Rd.
135
Taylor River
Almont
Taylor River Canyon Rd
Cement Creek Ranch
Campgrounds
Major highway
Divided highway
Dirt road
N
Gunnison
50
To Montrose
To Denver 200 mi.

in 1923, before Congress established the borders of the national forest. The eight cabins on the property were built in 1963, but only one is currently used as a rental.

Quiet and rugged it certainly is, and Cement Creek Ranch shouldn't be visited with anything but that in mind. This country is for the adventurer—in the best sense of the word—the person who enjoys the challenges of the great outdoors. Backpackers and hikers will find miles of trails and ridges to explore, and the nearby Taylor and Gunnison rivers offer big white-water runs for rafting and kayaking enthusiasts. Rock climbers will find some awesome granite climbs within walking distance. Overnight horsepack trips are guaranteed unforgettable experiences. For those less adventurous, the old-fashioned pool is probably the most enjoyable way to wallow away the time. Although the pool isn't really hot (about 75°F), the springs are moderately mineralized, and the bicarbonated water possesses diuretic and antacid properties.

It is highly unlikely that you would ever get bored in this rugged mountainous region along a branch of the Taylor River; however, you might get tired of cooking your own meals. There is no restaurant on the premises. In any case, a twelve-mile drive to the old mining town of Crested Butte is always an interesting diversion, and the little Victorian town is peppered with classy eateries.

You don't have to be an adventurer to enjoy Cement Creek Ranch, just someone who enjoys being someplace new and special. And if you enjoy wildlife (elk, mule deer, black bear, cougar, and mountain sheep), it sure beats south Denver.

Powderhorn or Cebolla Hot Springs

Gunnison County

Location: Thirty miles southwest of Gunnison on State Highway 149 in the city of Powderhorn, along Cebolla Creek
Elevation: 9,000 feet
Temperature: 100° to 106°F (38° to 41°C)
Flow: Unknown
Services: Thirteen cabins and store, bathhouse for guests only. Open May 15 to November.

Just off Highway 149 is a graded dirt road that leads to the little town of Powderhorn. The road is flat and dusty, and once you reach the end of it, you feel you've reached the end of the world. The town has a population of about seventy-five, along with one store and two gas pumps. A sign that says "cabins" leads you to a bridge crossing Cebolla Creek (state-stocked with good fishing). On your left you'll see two hand-hewn log cabins built over the springs; between them is a rickety outhouse. Straight ahead you'll see several cabins (all with wood-burning stoves) strung out along the base of a low-lying mountain. At one time a swimming pool was here, but today it's gone, and the area serves mainly as a hunting and fishing retreat.

During hunting season it's impossible to find lodging in Powderhorn. Regular customers have been coming here for decades, and there just isn't any room for newcomers. Early in the off-season it's possible to rent a cabin, but don't be surprised if you're treated with suspicion at first. The people here don't see many strangers, so sometimes the unexpected tourist is viewed as an invader. It's not that the townsfolk are unfriendly, it's just that they belong to a solid, permanent, and protective clan. For

Powderhorn Hot Springs.

almost a century the town has remained virtually the same. Land has been handed down from parent to child, and some people even live in the same houses their grandfathers built. There's tradition in this valley, and the locals would like to keep it that way. Nobody here really wants to see a high influx of tourists, because nobody wants to see Powderhorn lose its serenity.

Cebolla—a Spanish word meaning "onions"—Springs was named by the Spanish conquistadores, who probably found many wild onions growing in the valley. They also referred to the springs as *Ojo de Caballos*—Spring of the Horses. Early white settlers, who were unfamiliar with the Spanish language, renamed the springs Powderhorn. There are two stories that explain the origin of this name; the first is that one of the early settlers found a powderhorn here, and the second is that the valley itself is shaped like a powderhorn.

This is not real tourist country. It is a peaceful scenic valley, a valley with farms and simple folk, a valley without traffic jams, a valley that has resisted change. Beauty stretches out in all directions. Once you set eyes on the little frontier town, which somehow seems frozen in time, you can appreciate how the townsfolk feel.

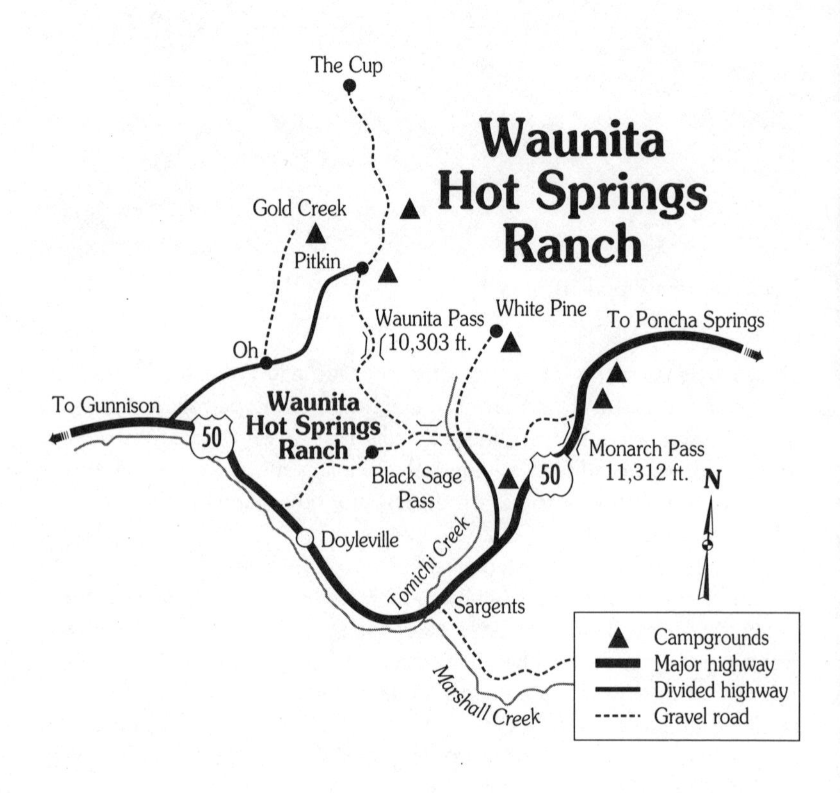

Waunita Hot Springs Ranch
The Cup
Gold Creek
Pitkin
Waunita Pass
10,303 ft.
White Pine
To Poncha Springs
Oh
To Gunnison
50
Waunita Hot Springs Ranch
Black Sage Pass
Monarch Pass
11,312 ft.
N
50
Doyleville
Tomichi Creek
Sargents
Marshall Creek
Campgrounds
Major highway
Divided highway
Gravel road

Waunita Hot Springs

Gunnison County

Waunita Hot Springs Ranch
8007 County Road 887
Gunnison, Colorado 81230
(303) 641-1266

Location: Nineteen miles east of Gunnison on Highway 50, then nine miles north of the village of Doyleville. There are two groups of springs about one-half mile apart on the south bank of Hot Springs Creek.
Elevation: 9,000 feet
Temperature: The hottest is 176°F (80°C)
Flow: 500 gallons per minute
Services: Fourteen family units, meals, horseback riding, fishing, hunting, game room, jeep tours. Reservations only; minimum stay of three days. Open all year.

Once in a very great while the traveler comes across the truly exceptional—a place with a wholesome appeal that is yet to be overrun. Such a place is Waunita Hot Springs Ranch, an eighty-acre guest ranch surrounded by the rolling, rugged wilderness of Gunnison National Forest.

There are two groups of springs in the area. Around the turn of the century, the water of the lower springs was bottled and shipped nationwide. Then, during the early 1920s, a fashionable resort was developed around the upper springs; at this time it was called the Waunita Hot Radium Springs. According to a report published in 1920 by the Colorado Geological Survey, "a large and well appointed hotel, sanitarium, bathhouse, plunges and other improvements" were built around the springs.

Today the Waunita Hot Springs Ranch is as impressive as it was back then, except that the emphasis is no longer on the hot springs.

Although the ranch has one of the nicest pools in the state (maintained at 95°F or 32°C) and all the ranch buildings are heated with geothermal energy, this is first and foremost a dude ranch—a friendly, informal working ranch.

Every summer day, experienced wranglers take guests on scenic riding trails that wind up to the high country. Along the way are hundreds of miles of virgin forest. Guided jeep tours are also available for those interested in exploring the old mining towns of North Star, White Pine, Pitkin, Tincup, and Woodstock. Sportsmen will find private lakes and streams stocked with rainbow, brown, and brook trout. In October and November one can hunt elk and deer (the ranch offers an all-inclusive hunting package). During the winter, the rolling landscape provides a perfect setting for cross-country skiing, sledding, and snowmobiling.

The meals here are extraordinary. Everything is served family-style and made from scratch (ham, oven-fried chicken, roast beef, steaks, fresh vegetables, fruit salads, and last but not least home-baked pies, cakes, and cobblers). In the morning you'll waken to the alluring smells of buttermilk biscuits baking in the oven and country bacon and sausage on the grill. And strong cowboy coffee is always on hand to start your motor churning.

The whole area is overflowing with western history (people are still finding Indian artifacts here). As a matter of fact, the mountain across from the lodge was named Tomichi Dome by the Utes. According to local historians, the Utes also named the springs. As the legend goes, an Indian maiden by the name of Waunita was buried at the foot of Tomichi Dome. She died after losing her lover in a bloody battle, and it's her warm tears that fill the springs.

After family-fun-filled days, you can retire to the reading room, take a dip in a mineral-water pool, or relax on the front porch, stargazing and listening to the night sounds. The ranch has an innocent beauty in an otherwise hectic world. Sitting here like this, you can almost see an Indian stalking wild game on the moonlit mountain in the distance.

Pinkerton Hot Springs

La Plata County

Location: Thirteen miles north of Durango on Route 550, along the south flank of the San Juan Mountains (Golden Horseshoe Resort)
Elevation: 7,000 feet
Temperature: 79° to 91°F (26° to 33°C)
Flow: 85 gallons per minute
Services: Not for public use

Pinkerton Hot Springs was once hidden in the densely forested Animas Valley, and like most hot springs situated at the flank of the San Juan Mountains, the mineral water flowed from a large fault. As recently as 1970, a quaint summer resort, complete with hot springs, mineral pool, cabins, and lodge stood proudly on this site. Today the resort is occupied by a private school, but the springs were entombed by a super highway (U.S. 550) in 1977. Colorado hot springs, like baby teeth, tend to disappear overnight.

Trimble Hot Springs

La Plata County

Trimble Hot Springs
6475 County Road 203
Durango, Colorado 81301
(303) 247-0111

Location: Six miles north of Durango off Highway 550 on Trimble Lane
Elevation: 6,600 feet
Temperature: 86° to 111°F (30° to 44°C)
Flow: Continuous flow-through
Services: Olympic-sized outdoor pool, outdoor therapy pool, indoor hydrojet pools, massage, body and skin treatments, physical therapy, acupuncture and other holistic healing treatments, aqua-aerobics, yoga classes, snack bar, picnic area, and fully equipped apartment with fireplace. Visa and MasterCard accepted.

When I first visited Trimble Hot Springs in the scenic Animas Valley in 1979, the old pool was empty. The water that once gushed from a fault at the base of a cliff had been reduced to a trickle, and the stone bathhouse had long since been abandoned. This was the same year the Bear family took ownership of the springs and began to develop a modern recreation center to rival any modern hot-spring resort in the state. In 1982, the flow of the mineral water was restored to what it once was, and the resort has been improving ever since.

This natural wonder was discovered by (who else?) W. F. Trimble in 1874. Trimble was a miserable Civil War veteran whose wretched body was twisted and bent by crippling arthritis. He thought that he was surely

Trimble Hot Springs in Durango.

doomed to a life of eternal pain until the day he took a bath in the natural hot spring. "Less than a month at the hot springs, and Trimble was a cured man," wrote Sandra Dallas, who described many historic water spots in her book, *No More than Five in a Bed.* It was Trimble's fabulous claims (he even claimed that the waters cured his tobacco habit) that first brought attention to the springs.

To make a long story short, Trimble built a boardinghouse at the springs. Later, a man by the name of Burns built a modest two-story hotel that burned down in the mid-1890s. A supposedly fireproof three-story hotel was built in its place. Ironically, that too burned down. The third hotel to be constructed on the spot catered mainly to Silverton miners, and with that, the reputation of the charming little resort began to slide. In the 1930s, Trimble Hot Springs was just another roadhouse filled with drunks, rowdies, gamblers, and other undesirables. In 1963 another violent fire roared through the building, and this time it was more than two decades before the springs would once again be open to the public. But it was worth the wait and definitely is worth a visit if you are ever in the Durango area.

Continental Divide Trail
To Del Norte
Archuleta Lake
Spotted Lake
Spruce Lakes
Hot Spring
Beaver Creek Trail
Rainbow Trail
Rainbow Hot Spring
Borns Lake
Sheep Mt.
Sheep Mt.
Treasure Pass
Treasure Falls
Silver Pass
Treasure Mt. Trail
Windy Pass
Silver Falls
Silver Creek Trail
Elwood Pass
Windy Pass Trail
160
667
East Fork
Continental Divide Trail
San Juan River
To Pagosa Springs
N
Campgrounds
Major highway
Divided highway
Gravel road

Rainbow/Wolf Creek Pass Hot Spring

Mineral County

Location: Just off Route 160 in the Weminuche Wilderness Area, eighteen miles northeast of Pagosa Springs. Four miles by trail from the West Fork trailhead.
Elevation: 10,000 feet
Temperature: 104°F (40°C)
Flow: 45 gallons per minute
Services: No services. Four miles from camping area. Check with the Rio Grande National Forest Service office before attempting this hike.

If you're planning a backpacking trip to Rainbow Hot Spring (known locally as Wolf Creek Pass Hot Spring), you've chosen the perfect place to be. Surrounded by the lush green forest of the Weminuche Wilderness Area, these two wilderness hot pots are outstanding among Colorado's many watering places, and one of the only undeveloped hot-spring areas still in recreational use in the state.

As U.S. 160 zigzags up over the back of Sheep Mountain toward Pagosa Springs, you'll see evidence of ice-age glaciation on the landscape. You'll also see outcroppings of grey shalelike rocks, which are ash beds left behind by a great volcano that erupted millions of years ago. When you reach the base of the pass, turn onto the dirt road that leads to the West Fork Campground. At the end of the road you'll find the Borns Lake cabin area. This is where the Rainbow Trail begins.

A strenuous four-mile hike takes you up the West Fork of the San Juan River, past Borns Lake, and eventually to the hot springs. Here the trail splits, and either branch you take will lead you to the Continental Divide Trail (about six more miles). The Beaver Creek Trail is the quickest route to Archuleta Lake, Spotted Lake, and Spruce Lakes. If you continue south on this trail, you'll eventually cross over Wolf Creek Pass (10,850 feet: get out your oxygen masks) and Treasure Pass. According to legend, back in 1790 a group of French miners hid $5 million in gold on this mountain after being driven out of the area by the Indians. The treasure was never recovered. If you travel north on the Continental Divide Trail (a few hundred miles), you'll eventually reach another hot-spring area—Steamboat Springs.

There is another story told about Wolf Creek Pass. At first the name conjures up images of the howling wilderness in Jack London's *Call of the Wild,* but Wolf Creek Pass wasn't named after the grey timber wolf; it was named after a man who was murdered up there. As the story goes, two pioneer cattlemen, Wolf and Sommers, had a quarrel concerning the cattle that they were transporting over the pass. The argument ended tragically. Wolf was shot between the eyes and died almost instantly. Sommers buried him under a big spruce tree near the creek in a crude coffin that he built from the sideboards of a wagon. It is said that Wolf's name is carved on that tree.

Reaching the hot spring—where warm steam rises like an elusive summons to paradise—is often frustrating to the backpacker. There is no sign telling you how high the San Juan River is running, and this is pertinent information if you plan on having a successful trip. Although the trail leads you over one rustic bridge, you eventually have to ford the San Juan River, and there are no ropes, cables, or logs to make the job easy. In early summer, and often later in the season, depending on the snowpack and runoff, it is next to impossible to reach the springs.

I remember my first trip. The first mile of the trail wandered through a thick forest sprinkled with about a half-dozen wilderness residences. Every few hundred feet there were signs that read: "Stay on Trail, Private Property," which gave me the uncomfortable feeling of walking through a stranger's backyard. But once this part of the trail was behind me, a primeval world seemed to unfold in the lush valleys of the Weminuche Wilderness. The chill in the morning air mingled with swarms of mosquitoes and the scent of pine. The trail led me through fields of ferns, which blanketed the forest floor and stood as tall as six feet, and along ridges of high cliffs overlooking the turbulent waters of the San Juan. When I finally reached the river crossing, I knew I was in for one of nature's great challenges. I stepped into the freezing waist-deep water and was nearly swept downstream. I never did make it to the spring that day. It's just one of those disappointments that are too familiar to the backpacker who tries to reach Rainbow Hot Spring.

I once heard someone say: "You can visit the hot spring only if the river lets you visit the hot spring." This is true, though your chances are best after mid-July. It was late in August the day I made it up to the spring, and though the volume of water that the San Juan carried was probably the lowest it had been all year, the mighty river was still difficult to ford. After I had safely reached the other side, it seemed like no time at all and the trail led me to another river crossing: Beaver Creek is somewhat narrower than the San Juan River, but the crossing is just as perilous. At this point the trail became steep, and I still had about two more miles to go.

The sky grew dark, it thundered, and by the time I reached the spring, the forest swayed in a squall-like downpour. Trout might have swum through the air, and it seemed improbable that I could hike back through it to the safety of my car. Drenched and shivering, I stood on a high ridge, looking down at the muddy river that seemed to be rising by the minute. Two hundred feet below me I could see the spring flowing from a fissure in the side of a cliff into the two terraced rock pools. I glissaded down the slick canyon wall toward the steaming spring. Here I soaked in the warm water and waited for the storm to let up. But the rain kept falling. I listened uneasily to the sound of the wind ripping through the trees, haunted by the vision of rising water. Then I realized that once again I would have to surrender to the river.

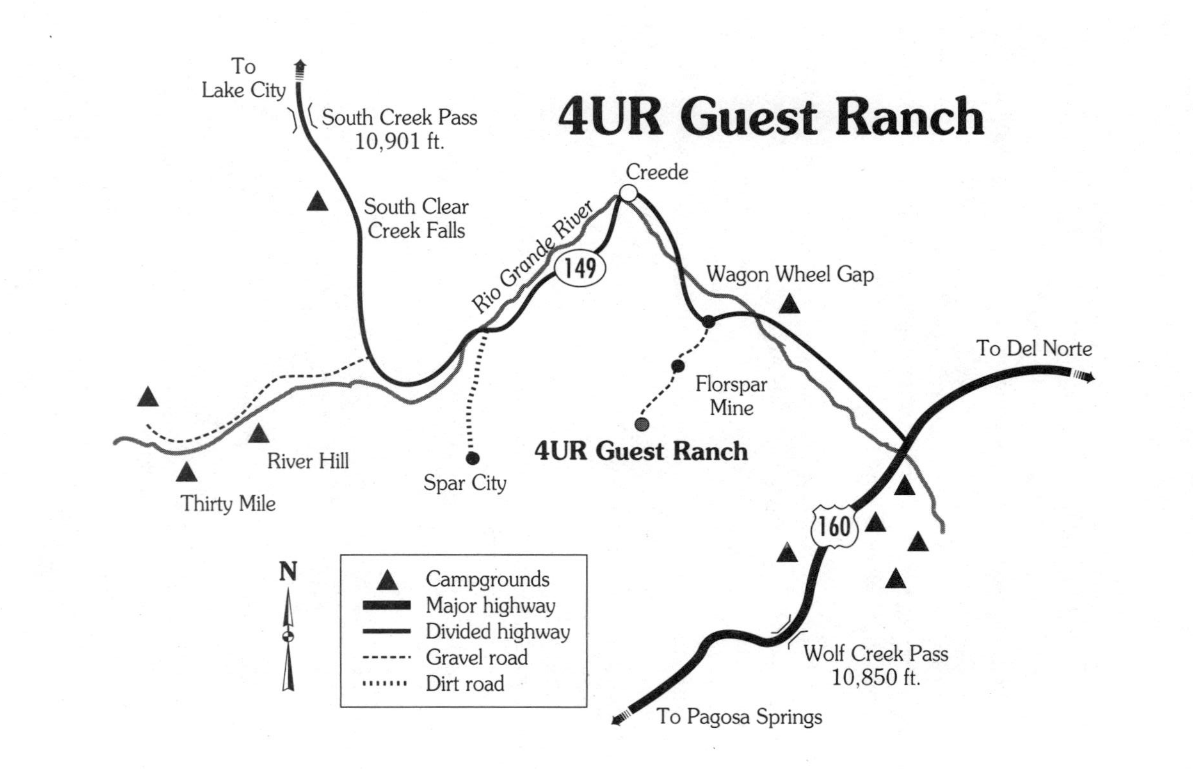
4UR Guest Ranch
To
Lake City
South Creek Pass
10,901 ft.
South Clear
Creek Falls
Creede
Rio Grande River
149
Wagon Wheel Gap
To Del Norte
Florspar
Mine
4UR Guest Ranch
River Hill
Thirty Mile
Spar City
160
N
Campgrounds
Major highway
Divided highway
Gravel road
Dirt road
Wolf Creek Pass
10,850 ft.
To Pagosa Springs

Wagon Wheel Gap Hot Springs

Mineral County

4UR Guest Ranch
Box 340
Creede, Colorado 81130
(719) 658-2202

Location: Ten miles south of Creede on Route 149 to Wagon Wheel Gap. Follow signs to the ranch.
Elevation: 8,400 feet
Temperature: 131° to 134°F (55° to 57°C)
Flow: 50 gallons per minute
Services: No credit cards. Rooms, ranch store, meals, horseback riding, tennis. Reservations only. Minimum of one week stay. Open June 1 through November 15.

Early in the spring, if you drive into Wagon Wheel Gap it looks like a ghost town. Rustic log cabins dot the highway like seeds in a watermelon, and all seem empty and lonely this time of the year. In the summer it's another story. Tourists from all over the country flock to the area, and during July and August it's often impossible to find lodging here. One of the most popular resorts is the 4UR Guest Ranch.

About a mile west of town is a dirt road that runs south, crosses the railroad tracks, takes you through a frontier gate, and eventually leads you to the ranch. Once you're there, you'll realize why this is one of the most exclusive dude ranches in the state. Set in a high valley along Goose Creek, the ranch is surrounded by Rio Grande National Forest. Miles of high mountain trails lead to peaks with inspiring vistas—truly a western wonderland.

Historical photograph of Wagon Wheel Gap Hot Springs. *(Courtesy Colorado Historical Society)*

After a hard day in the saddle, a dip in the pool (maintained at 78°F or 25.5°C) is always a welcome relief. But if your aquatic tastes tend to extravagance, the indoor jet pool is guaranteed to induce a sense of quiet luxury previously known only to kings.

There are four other hot springs and one cold spring bubbling up along Goose Creek; the largest is Boiling Springs. Hot Soda Spring, Hot Sulphur Spring, Hot Saline Spring, and Cold Lithia Spring are the others. These springs aren't used for recreation, and it will take some serious exploring to locate them.

The first bathhouse was built in 1902, and though it is no longer used, the ornate building still stands like a testament to the old days. For its first few years of operation, the spa attracted people from all over the country, but it was never a financial success.

Today the 4UR is one of the most successful dude ranches in Colorado. This three-thousand-acre spread has seven miles of private, well-stocked trout streams, two miles of river fishing, and a lake. Knowledgeable guides are always on hand to help you improve your riding skills, or to lead you on pack trips deep into the wilderness where the forests and meadows are teeming with more than seventy kinds of animals. If you remember the Walt Disney movie *Cougar Country*, you already have a good idea of what it's like at the ranch. According to the 4UR's brochure, this is where the Disney crew lived and filmed the movie.

Everything you need for the ultimate western vacation is right here; you'll never have to leave. The food is excellent, whether it be the chuck-wagon cookouts or your daily catch prepared by one of the chefs and served with a flair in the spacious dining room. There is no end to what the ranch has to offer: jeep rides into the high country, pack trips, hunting packages, recreation room with ping pong and billiards, spa, modern accommodations. This is definitely a rancho deluxe.

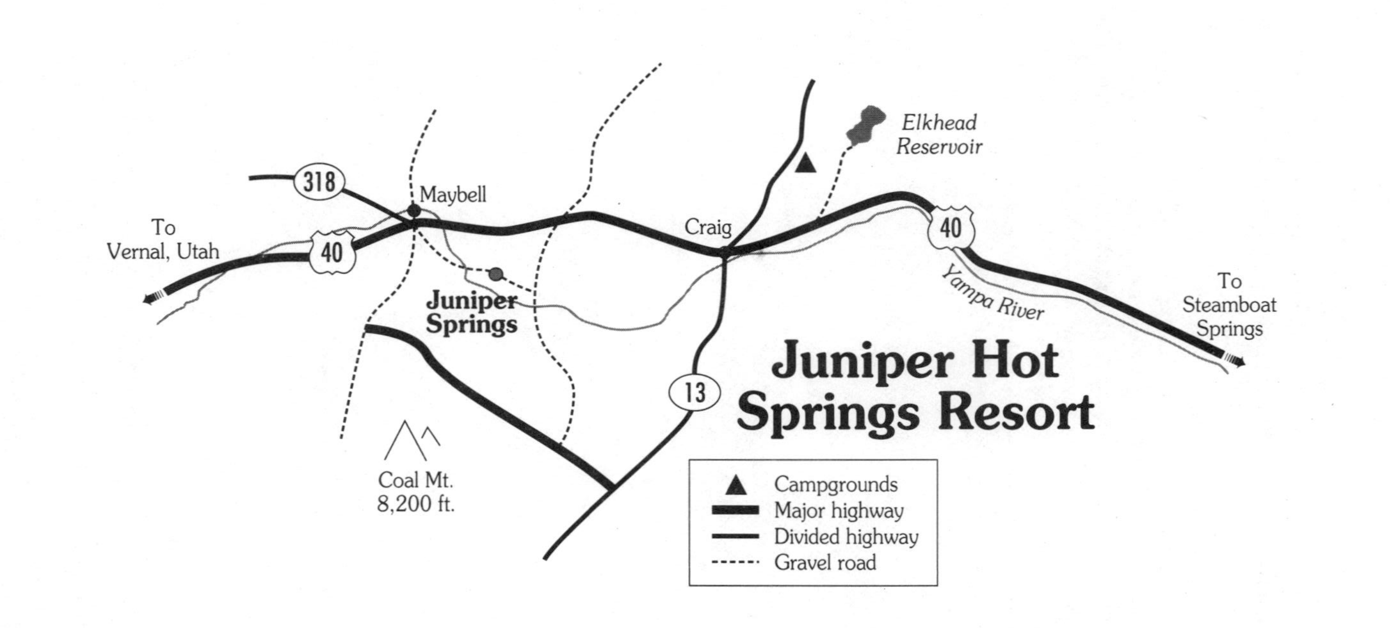
Juniper Hot Springs Resort
Elkhead Reservoir
318
Maybell
To Vernal, Utah
40
Craig
40
Yampa River
To Steamboat Springs
Juniper Springs
13
Coal Mt. 8,200 ft.
Campgrounds
Major highway
Divided highway
Gravel road

Juniper Hot Springs

Moffat County

Juniper Hot Springs Resort
8090 County Road 53
Craig, Colorado 81625

Location: Twenty-two miles west of Craig on U.S. 40, then five miles south on County Road 53
Elevation: 6,000 feet
Temperature: 91° to 99°F (33° to 37°C)
Flow: Combined flow approximately 50 gallons per minute

On the south shore of the Yampa River is a cluster of low decrepit buildings that look small and lonesome under the big sky. Here on this arid, empty land is what remains of the Juniper Springs Resort. Not too long ago Stella Craig, the owner of the property, advertised the therapeutic properties of the water. Her business card read: "Springs noted for relief of Arthritis, Polio, Hives and other toxic Ailments." But in 1990, Stella closed the tiny resort. "I simply got too old to run it," she said.

Ever since the early 1920s, Juniper Hot Springs has enjoyed a faithful following of visitors, but recently it has grown dingy and seedy. There is a reason for this: The resort is for sale. Stella says she hopes whoever buys the place respects and understands the history and the curative powers of the water.

The history Stella refers to goes back to the 1870s. According to local legend, this is when the first white man discovered the springs. By accident he stumbled upon two moccasins beside what looked like a large hole used by badgers. He peered into the tunnel and saw a steaming hot spring in the filtered light. He spread the word, and soon after, a small bathhouse was built over the springs. As more and more people began to visit the springs, more substantial accommodations were constructed—hotel, dining room, and livery stable. Today the complex awaits its future.

The hot springs are located in the floodplain of the Yampa River. The sodium bicarbonate water percolates up through shales and sandstones from the Cretaceous period. No one really knows what's going to become of the Juniper Hot Springs Resort. But maybe, just maybe, it will reopen to the public and once again enjoy a faithful following of health seekers.

Ridgway Hot Springs or Orvis Hot Springs

Ouray County

Orvis Hot Springs
1585 County Road #3
Ridgway, Colorado 81432
(303) 626-5324

Location: Eight and one-half miles north of Ouray and one and one-half miles south of Ridgway on U.S. 550
Elevation: 6,900 feet
Temperature: 127°F (53°C)
Flow: Unknown
Services: Indoor pool, three private indoor soaking pools, natural outdoor pool, hot-rock sauna, six guest rooms, and six camping spaces. Visa and MasterCard accepted. Open all year.

Simple as a nail, this charming hot-spring resort is an ideal place to get away from it all. Ten years ago this was a chiropractic and hydrotherapy center. Today it is more of a hot-spring retreat, a place to relax and soak your worries away. The large outdoor soaking pool is about six feet deep and thirty feet in diameter, with hot mineral water continuously bubbling up from the bottom. Large stones surround this natural hot spring and accentuate the lovely natural setting. The rooms are kept scrupulously clean. The sodium sulfate water here has a high concentration of iron, and the formed concrete tubs, all painted bright yellow, give the place a spotless, functional look. Robes and towels are supplied. Clothing is optional in all pools except the indoor pool.

Orvis Hot Springs in Ridgway.

The guest rooms at Orvis Hot Springs.

Orvis Hot Springs is situated in a vast, wide-open valley where the climate is dry and cool. If you look south toward Ouray, you'll see the entire Dallas Range looming on the horizon like the upturned blade of a ripsaw. Don't be surprised if you have a sudden déjà vu experience while viewing this majestic scene, for you've undoubtedly seen it many times before. The valley has been used as a backdrop in many classic Hollywood Westerns, such as *True Grit* and *How the West Was Won*.

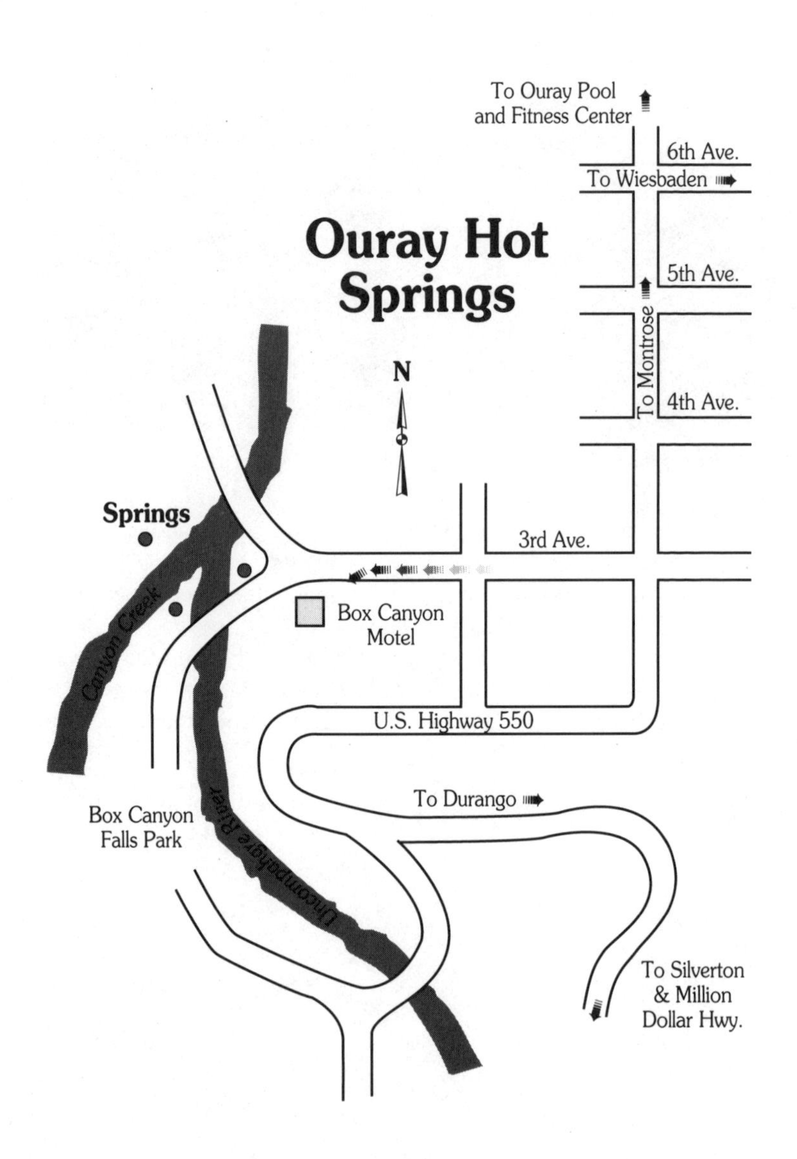
To Ouray Pool
and Fitness Center
6th Ave.
To Wiesbaden
Ouray Hot
Springs
5th Ave.
To Montrose
N
4th Ave.
Springs
3rd Ave.
Box Canyon
Motel
Canyon Creek
U.S. Highway 550
To Durango
Box Canyon
Falls Park
Uncompahgre River
To Silverton
& Million
Dollar Hwy.

Ouray Hot Springs

Ouray County

Location: Numerous springs are scattered throughout the town of Ouray
Elevation: 7,800 feet
Temperature: 86° to 156°F (30° to 69°C)
Flow: 5 to 200 gallons per minute
Services: Picnicking, hiking

My favorite hot springs in Colorado and almost the entire world are in Ouray. I never get tired of looking at the pristine landscape, certainly the most beautiful in the world.

A quaint little alpine village (800 people) surrounded by the high peaks of the San Juan Mountains and the Uncompahgre National Forest, Ouray has rightfully earned the title of the "Switzerland of America."

This is a place for hot-spring lovers who'd rather not see so many other hot-spring lovers when they go hot-spring-hopping. Down along Canyon Creek and the Uncompahgre River you'll find a multitude of springs bubbling up into small rock pools. This is truly a hot-pot paradise; however, soaking in these pools is discouraged.

To reach these springs, make a right turn off Third Street onto the last street (Third Avenue), going south out of town. Follow the signs on the gravel road past the Box Canyon Motel until you come to a small parking area. From here there are a number of trails leading to Box Canyon Park, where you'll find many springs seeping up along the bank of the creek. There are three groups of springs in the area, which are estimated to contain over one hundred individual sulfated springs. The majority of these springs are highly mineralized and radioactive. As a matter of fact,

Historical photograph of the rest house in Box Canyon. *(Courtesy Colorado Historical Society)*

the whole group of springs was once referred to as the Radio Active Mineral Springs.

The visitor has the feeling of being in a remote part of the world, especially in the springs, even when you're only a few blocks from the center of town. White-capped mountains tower above, looking ridiculously like gigantic Dairy Queen cones. This is very special country indeed.

This late-Victorian mining town was named after the Ute chieftain who was responsible for bringing peace between prospectors and the Ute tribes. One historian said that Ouray (pronounced you-ray) means arrow, but Chief Ouray himself said that it was just the first word he spoke as a baby.

In 1875 the first white men, A. W. Beogle and Jack Eckles, entered the area; that same year they discovered the Cedar and Clipper lodes. A month later the Fisherman and Trout lodes were discovered. Word leaked, and a wild stampede of miners headed toward Ouray. By the winter of 1876, the town had grown to a population of 400; by 1880 the population soared to a staggering 2,669.

The town prospered as never before. The railroad arrived in 1888. Then, in 1896, the richest discovery in the town's history was unearthed. Thomas Walsh's Camp Bird Mine produced more than $26 million in less than two decades, and the new tycoon was so wealthy that he purchased the famous Hope Diamond for his daughter. But eventually the momentum of mining slowed, and today tourism is the town's most important industry.

The hop from Ouray to Silverton (twenty-five miles) takes about half an hour. Visitors who have made the short trip on the so-called Million Dollar Highway generally say that the adventure was worthwhile—but an adventure it most definitely is. The road was built by Otto Mears in 1883. Some say that the highway is constructed with mine tailings containing more than a million dollars worth of gold; others say that back in 1922 (when improvements were being made for automobiles), the three-mile stretch of road between Ouray and Ironton cost a million dollars to build—$1.2 million to be exact. Numerous hairpin turns lead up over Red Mountain Pass and past the ghost towns of Ironton Park and Red Mountain. Keep your eyes open for hot springs; you just might discover one that nobody knows about. About five miles out of Silverton, you'll see a sea of algae flowing down the side of a mountain on the right side of the road. This isn't a warm spring—it's seepage from a warm-water well located high above the road. Nevertheless, it's evidence that there is thermal activity in the area.

Whenever I'm in Ouray, I dine at the Outlaw on Third Street, an excellent restaurant with a superb wine list. I go to the Longbranch, across the street, to play pool and drink beer. The boisterous, ribald atmosphere is amusing, but one has to be in exactly the right frame of mind for this.

In the 1920s a number of bathing establishments flourished in this area. Back then, many of the springs had names like Pavilion Spring, Fish Spring, Bath House Spring, Big Springs, and Cougar Spring. Today most of the springs are nameless (feel free to name one after yourself), and there are only three hot-spring spas still in business.

If you have a few days to spend in Ouray, here are a few available attractions that are well worth the visit: Box Canyon Falls, the Ouray historical walking tour, Chipeta Movie Theater, the historic St. Elmo Hotel with the popular Bon Ton Restaurant downstairs, an assortment of unusual shops and stores, and the museum. For the outdoor adventurer, the opportunities are endless: hunting, fishing, backpacking, jeeping, hiking, photography, tennis, rafting, picnicking, snowmobiling, snowshoeing, cross-country skiing, downhill skiing, rockhounding, and roller skating.

Ouray Hot Springs

Ouray County

Box Canyon Motel
45 Third Avenue
Ouray, Colorado 81427
(303) 325-4981

Location: At the end of Third Avenue in the town of Ouray
Elevation: 7,700 feet
Temperature: 120°F (49°C)
Flow: Numerous springs with mineral seeps are located at the rear of the motel
Services: Thirty rooms, color TV, telephones, two spring-fed hot tubs. All major credit cards accepted.

(See map on page 106.)

In this horn-honking, computerized, paper-pushing world, it's nice to know that a place like the Box Canyon Motel exists. Nothing extraordinary, it's just a nice place to stay in one of the nicest areas in the world. The Uncompahgre (Ute for "hot water") River is within easy walking distance. There are miles of hiking trails wandering along the awesome Box Canyon. Only 21 feet wide, the canyon rises 221 feet above the valley floor and is spanned by a footbridge.

Colorado sportsmen—especially jeepers and trail-bikers—already know about the several hundred miles of wilderness roads. Jeep rental is available nearby. Is there any other way to spend a vacation than to four-wheel it back to a good fishing spot? Hook a few, fry a few. Head back to the motel for a hot-spring cocktail in a California-style redwood hot tub (five feet around and four feet deep). Hit the sack early. Get up early and do it all over again.

Historical photograph of the exterior of Box Canyon. *(Courtesy Colorado Historical Society)*

Ouray Hot Springs

Ouray County

Ouray Pool and Fitness Center
For information, contact:
Ouray Chamber of Commerce
Ouray, Colorado 81427
(303) 325-4638

Location: U.S. 550 at Tenth Avenue; north end of town
Temperature: 156°F (69°C)
Flow: Water pumped from Box Canyon and mixed with cold city water
Services: Fitness center, locker rooms, swim shop with suit rentals, massage therapy, snack bar, and picnic tables. Admission fee. Visa and MasterCard accepted. Open all year.

(See map on page 106.)

This large municipal swimming pool (250 feet long and 150 feet wide) is the first thing you'll see when you drive into the town of Ouray from Ridgway. "Impressive," "awesome," "breathtaking" are just a few of the adjectives that have been used to describe its beauty. This is the town's main attraction, and it's no wonder why.

The people of Ouray worked hard for their pool. A brochure circulated by the Ouray Chamber of Commerce tells the story: "In 1920 the people of Ouray expressed a desire for a Mineral Hot Spring Pool . . . the site decided on was the Radium Springs Park north of town . . . In 1926 the pool was constructed from local volunteer help. The first dressing rooms were wooden side rails and floor, and tent tops. In 1929 a frame structure was built to house the office and dressing rooms."

Historical photograph of Ouray from Radium Springs Park. *(Courtesy Colorado Historical Society)*

The modern facility you see today was built in 1974 and completely remodeled in 1983. It is the largest pool in southwest Colorado. Flanked on the east by a large goldfish pond, the oval-shaped pool goes from two to nine feet in depth.

The pool is supplied with a calcium sulfate mineral water from a spring located at the upper reaches of Box Canyon. This water is piped clear across town. According to the Environmental Protection Agency, this water isn't fit to drink. However, the water gushes from the spring at a rate of about 200 gallons per minute, and when it arrives at the pool it is mixed with cool city water, bringing the temperature to a comfortable 95°F. It's a hot-spring Shangri-la, except without palm trees.

The Ouray Pool and Fitness Center.

Ouray Hot Springs

Ouray County

Wiesbaden Spa
Box 349
Ouray, Colorado 81427
(303) 325-4347

Location: Corner of Sixth Avenue and Fifth Street in the town of Ouray
Temperature: 86° to 127°F (30° to 53°C)
Flow: 2 to 30 gallons per minute
Services: Eighteen rooms, kitchenettes available, no phone, outdoor pool (no chlorine), vapor cave, picnic area. Credit cards accepted. Open all year.

(See map on page 106.)

Imagine swimming in a hot-spring-fed pool on a snowy evening, with puffy flakes falling straight down onto the surface of the steaming water. Imagine yourself floating peacefully. Thick fog enshrouds you, rising like a gigantic ghost into the night, obscuring the snow. But you can feel the tiny flakes dancing upon your face and eyelids. That's what it's like at the Wiesbaden Motel and Health Spa.

At first glance it appears to be your basic motel, but a closer look reveals the spa's uniqueness. In the basement of the building and hewn into the side of a rock mountain is a vapor cave. One of the owners told me that this particular grotto was the inspiration for Hugh Hefner's famous pleasure pool at his Los Angeles mansion. Water from one of the four springs, which provides space heating for the rooms (a comfortable seventy degrees) and water for the outdoor pool, seeps in through a wall in the cavern. Millions of tiny particles have formed a smooth, slippery coating of minerals on the floor and the bulging rock walls. Bathers sit on a concrete bench around the sides of the eight-foot by twelve-foot pool, which is maintained at 106°F. The cave was discovered by miners who were tunneling for gold back in the 1800s, and it has functioned as a spa ever since 1918.

Lodge guests have unlimited use of all facilities (sauna, showers, exercise room). The public is welcome for a modest fee. The equipment is modern, and exercise rooms are clean and carpeted. Other spa amenities include cross-country ski lessons and tours, professional masseuse and masseur, reflexology, acupressure, facials, salt rubs, exercise classes, and snowshoe rental and sales. This is a good spa for families and for those who are interested in health and fitness.

Hartsel Hot Springs

Park County

Location: Southern end of Park County. Adjacent to U.S. 24 in the town of Hartsel. Ask at the South Park Mercantile.
Elevation: 8,860 feet
Temperature: 113° to 126°F (45° to 52°C)
Flow: 100 gallons per minute
Services: None. Close to the town of Hartsel. Status unknown; inquire locally.

This free attraction, located on the southern edge of the little town of Hartsel (named after the pioneer cattleman Sam Hartsel) is not a hot spring that I recommend you go out of your way to visit. But if you are a tightfisted traveler rolling along the range on U.S. 24 looking for a cheap place to take a bath, this just might be the spot for you. But don't expect anything fancy, for what was once a fashionable spa is now a ramshackle memory. The main bathhouse, which stands dark and empty and is under siege by rural vandals, is slowly decaying. The masseurs and masseuses have long since vanished; some believe that they've been eaten by mosquitoes.

As you approach the spring, you'll see three dilapidated buildings flanked by the Mosquito Mountains on the west and surrounded by a bright blue swamp. These springs are highly radioactive, which contributes to the intense heat of the water and the iridescent blue color in the well-known barite deposit a few miles away.

Inside a rickety one-room shed built over one of the springs you'll find an old enameled bathtub and a couple of large plastic buckets. Go ahead, nobody minds if you take a bath here, although there is a certain bathing

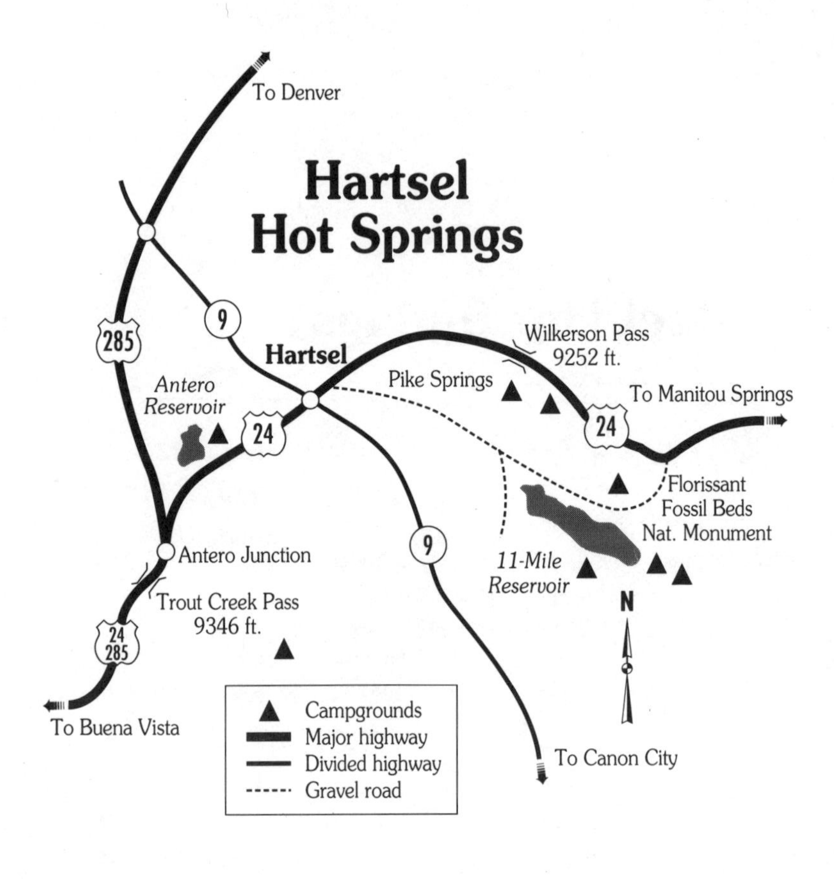
Hartsel
Hot Springs
To Denver
285
9
Hartsel
Wilkerson Pass
9252 ft.
Pike Springs
To Manitou Springs
Antero
Reservoir
24
Florissant
Fossil Beds
Nat. Monument
Antero Junction
9
11-Mile
Reservoir
Trout Creek Pass
9346 ft.
N
24
285
To Buena Vista
Campgrounds
Major highway
Divided highway
Gravel road
To Canon City

etiquette that should be followed. When you enter, you should find one of the plastic buckets already filled with cold water. Plug the tub and pour in the cold water. Then fill the rest of the tub with buckets of 135°F water scooped from a hole in the floor of the shed until you get the temperature you want. Now you're ready for a real pioneer bath. Slowly ease into the water. Ahhh! Where else in this raw land can we relax in an antique tub as grasshoppers whirr outside the door and summon up remembrances of the old frontier?

Before you go, leave a bucket of hot water to cool for the next person, and don't forget to close the gate so that the cattle won't get out.

Rhodes Warm Spring

Park County

Location: Omitted by request of owner
Elevation: 9,900 feet
Temperature: 77°F (25°C)
Flow: 250 gallons per minute

This group of privately owned hot springs was once used by the Boy Scouts back in 1910. The old bathhouse has since been torn down, and now the springs are used to raise trout. The tepid water is perfect for raising fingerlings (baby rainbow trout) because the water only drops to about 65°F in the winter. The fish don't freeze, so they grow about ten to twelve inches in a year. Because the owner doesn't want to be bothered with trespassers swimming in his trout ponds, this is all the information that is available.

Conundrum Hot Springs

Pitkin County

Location: From the town of Aspen, take Route 82 west five miles to Castle Creek Road. Turn left and go four and one-half miles north. Then take a primitive dirt road three miles to the trailhead. Nine miles by trail.
Elevation: 11,200 feet
Temperature: 100°F (38°C)
Flow: 50 gallons per minute
Services: Obtain information from the Forest Service office in Aspen before attempting this hike. Cross-country skiers should check avalanche conditions. Open June 1 to September 15.

The unmarked dirt road runs south along Conundrum Creek, winding through a forest of fir and aspen trees. You're headed toward the Snowmass Wilderness Area. Three miles and a thousand chuckholes later you'll reach a dusty, primitive parking lot. This is where the Conundrum Springs trail begins. From here on in, the only things that matter are the pack on your back, the clouds in the sky, and that rocky ribbon of trail ahead.

The journey to Conundrum is like living a scene out of *Grizzly Adams*. Everything is so beautiful and unspoiled, and that's why people come here: for the sun, the mountains, and the sky as blue as a robin's egg. The trail meanders through a valley, appropriately named Avalanche Valley. Sometimes in the summer you can hear small but usually harmless rock slides echoing off the mountain slopes. In the winter this place can be dangerous, and anyone who attempts to cross-country ski to the springs should first check avalanche conditions. Of course, the safest way to travel is with an experienced guide. Nordic Adventures of Crested Butte offers overnight ski trips to the springs that will take you through

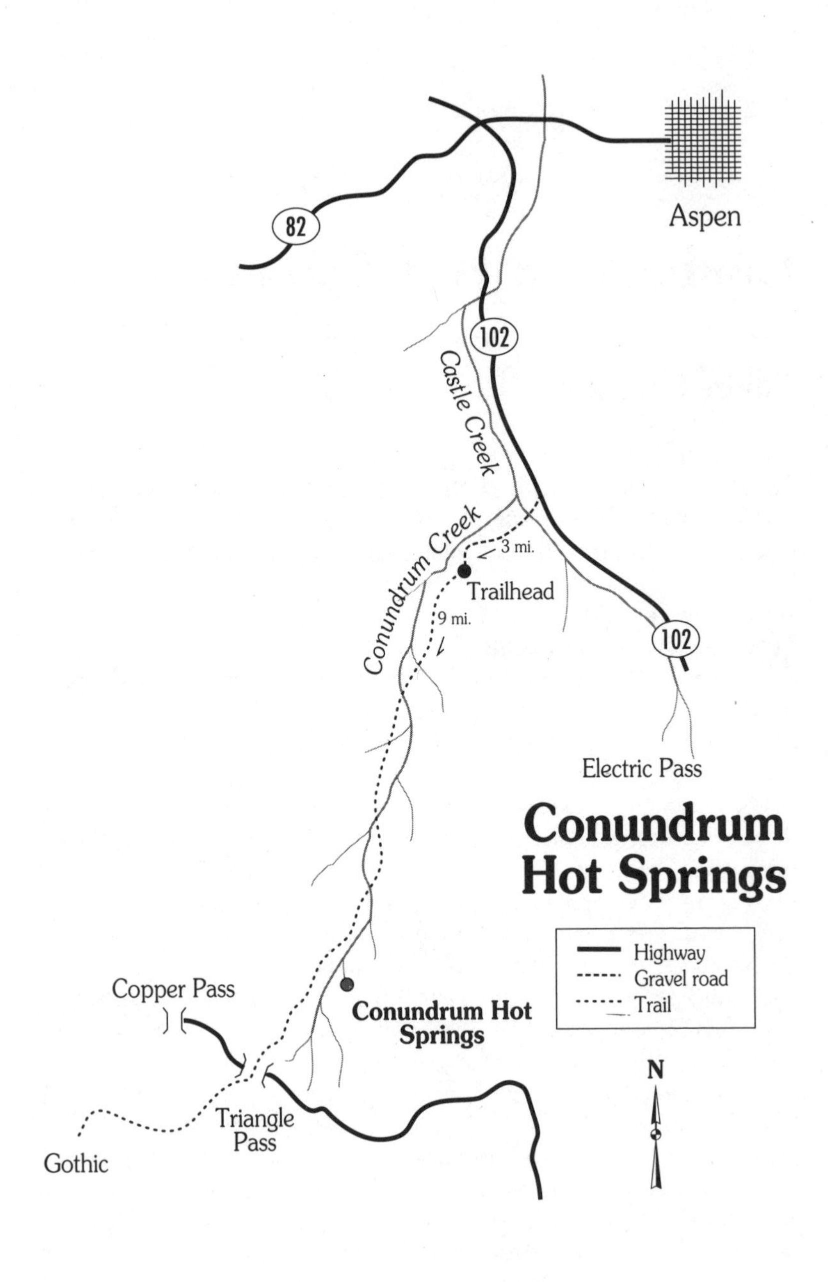

82
Aspen
102
Castle Creek
Conundrum Creek
3 mi.
Trailhead
9 mi.
102
Electric Pass
Conundrum
Hot Springs
Highway
Gravel road
Trail
Copper Pass
Conundrum Hot
Springs
N
Triangle
Pass
Gothic

the old mining town of Gothic, up over a 13,000-foot pass, and eventually down to the springs, where you'll camp for the night. The white powder snow up here is the same snow that is in Aspen—perhaps better—which makes for the ultimate Nordic ski experience. Imagine waking up in the morning and poking your head out of your snow shelter: The sky is sunrise pink. Winter solitude surrounds you. There are no lift lines, no drugged, crazed loonies to contend with; just miles and miles of glistening untracked snow. This is winter at its best.

But the best of summer can also be experienced up at Conundrum once you get to the springs, which is easier said than done. The trail is deceiving. The first three miles are flat and easy to hike, but then the trail becomes steep and strenuous. Eventually you have to cross the creek not once but three times. There are no footbridges along the trail, only fallen trees. In the early spring, when the white water is running high and fast, these crossings may seem rather frightening. But don't think about danger, exhaustion, or the painful blisters on your feet. Fix your mind instead on how wonderful it's going to feel to soothe your aching, tired muscles in a steamy hot spring.

This is true paradise. Come sundown, the mountains turn golden. From here you can look out over the whole valley, and it seems as if you've reached the end of the rainbow. Later, the summer night entertains you with the beauty of thousands of stars.

The only problem with this particular paradise is that it is quite popular, especially in midsummer, and sometimes there just aren't enough springs to go around. Unfortunately, there are only two springs of considerable size. The main pool measures approximately ten feet by eight feet and is about three feet deep. The second pool, which is fed by the main pool, is somewhat larger—ten feet by ten feet—and is about five feet deep. The other springs are hardly more than shallow rock pools for soaking trail-weary feet.

During the height of the summer season, communal soaking is quite common, and so is nudity, for this is where the beautiful people of Aspen go to rid themselves of their chic apparel. All in all, the scene is mellow. Those who want privacy keep to themselves, and those who like to socialize can usually find some friendly folks to share their experiences with.

Mostly the people up here are nature lovers, and they romp through the mountain meadows on their little cat's feet, clomp, clomp, clomp, without realizing that the fragile ecosystem is being broken under their heavy tread. The Forest Service has prohibited camping within one mile of the springs in an attempt to protect the alpine vegetation, yet people continue to rip branches from the few trees for firewood and bough beds. These few people could turn Conundrum into a lost paradise, a fool's paradise. Not only is the environment being damaged, but it's also unsafe for camping. The area just above the springs is called Electric Pass, because the massive iron ore deposits up there attract lightning. If you value life, it's best to seek out one of the many pleasant campsites in the forest below.

Conundrum is a spring for all seasons; but if you want to avoid the crowds, it's a good idea to restrict your visit to weekdays either in the early spring or autumn. If you're adventurous and strong, winter might be your choice. Whichever you choose, you'll find the Elk Mountains, in the Snowmass-Maroon Bells Wilderness, some of the most colorful country in the world—whether it be the pastel spring butterflies in contrast to the towering evergreens, the shimmering yellow of the autumn aspens against the backdrop of a crisp blue sky, or a cloud of white snow as it billows down the side of a rock cliff. The pristine beauty of this area is always impressive.

Penny Hot Springs

Pitkin County

Location: Twelve miles south of Carbondale on Route 133, along the banks of the Crystal River.
Elevation: 6,181 feet
Temperature: 104° to 133°F (40° to 56°C)
Flow: 200 gallons per minute

Between Redstone and Glenwood Springs on Highway 133 is a cartridge belt full of hot springs running along both banks of the Crystal River. Stretching nearly a half-mile upstream, the largest group of springs is located three miles north of Redstone. Although the area was once named Avalanche Hot Springs because of snowslides that plague the area, many people have chosen to build their homes in this scenic valley. Many of the springs are located on private property, and those that aren't run adjacent to private property. So if you're determined to go exploring, don't expect any privacy, and remember that you just might be depriving the local residents of *their* privacy.

According to Lloyd E. Parris, who did considerable research on this area for his authoritative book *Caves of Colorado,* a thermal cave is located along the bank of the Crystal River. Parris unearthed an article from an 1889 edition of the *Denver Times,* "Caves on the Western Slope." According to the article, "Hot Springs is located about twelve miles from Carbondale on the Line of the Crystal River Railroad," the exact location of Penny Hot Springs.

This five-room cavern was discovered by a group of miners who blasted into the steaming inferno by accident. Like a fire-breathing dragon, the cave's toothy mouth yawned, exposing stone jaws laden with sparkling crystal stalactites and stalagmites. Soon a large number of health seekers, attracted to the medicinal properties of the water, visited the cavern. The Crystal River Railroad promoted the idea of building a "commodious" bathhouse, swimming pool, and hotel to rival that of Glenwood Springs, but the cavern didn't sustain the interest of the public, and it began almost immediately its slide back into quiescence.

Parris concluded: "Assuming this location being correct and if the tunnel is still enterable, the caverns should be easily found because the Redstone topographical map shows only two mines in the area." Let us know if you find it.[1]

Notes

1. Lloyd E. Parris, *Caves of Colorado* (Boulder, Colo.: Pruett Press, Inc., 1973), p. 15.

Don K Ranch Springs

Pueblo County

Don K Ranch
2677 South Siloam Road
Pueblo, Colorado 81004
(719) 784-6600

Location: Nineteen and one-half miles west of Pueblo on Highway 96, then south six miles to ranch
Elevation: 6,000 feet
Temperature: 82°F (28°C)
Flow: 25 gallons per minute
Services: Twenty-three units, meals, horseback riding, hiking, skeet shooting, game room. Reservations only. Open May 15 through November 15.

About twenty miles west of Pueblo, I turned onto a dirt road and bounced up toward the Don K Ranch. The six-mile road that twisted through Red Creek Canyon was a mess—rutted and almost washed out in some places. Just before I reached the first creek crossing, I noticed a sign nailed to a tree: "You think this is bad, you ought to try driving in the winter." With that reassuring thought in mind, I ventured onward, but when I came to the second creek crossing, I lost my nerve, parked the car, and walked the rest of the way.

Seeing the Don K Ranch for the first time is like walking onto the set of *Bonanza*. Giant ponderosa pines tower over the corrals, barns, the bunkhouse, guest houses, and the magnificent log lodge. In the distance,

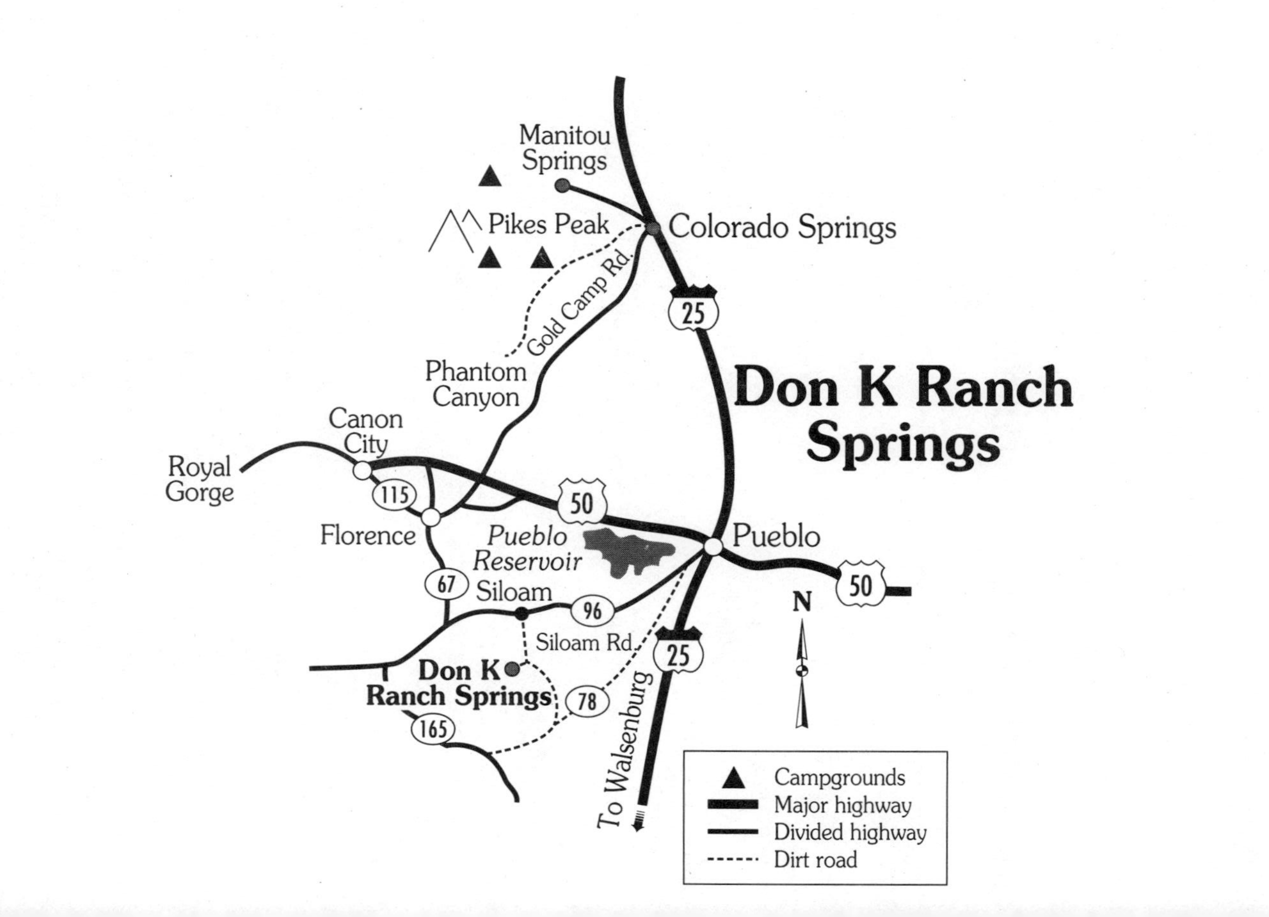
Don K Ranch Springs
Manitou Springs
Pikes Peak
Colorado Springs
25
Gold Camp Rd.
Phantom Canyon
Canon City
Royal Gorge
115
Florence
50
Pueblo Reservoir
Pueblo
67
Siloam
96
Siloam Rd.
Don K Ranch Springs
78
165
To Walsenburg
N
Campgrounds
Major highway
Divided highway
Dirt road

a small herd of about twenty horses played on the high grassy range while the wranglers tried rounding them up for the evening.

Although the ranch is nestled in a quiet valley in the Wet Mountains (so named because of the multitude of springs and creeks that flow in this lush region), it has no hot mineral-water pool; however, it does have an attractive king-sized pool (heated and filtered and fed by pure mountain springs) surrounded by umbrella tables and complete with shuffleboard. Buffet lunches and moonlight dances are often held poolside.

The trails on this spread not only take you through open meadows, colorful canyons, and deep mountain forests, but also take you back in time. Just above the ranch is an old wagon road leading to a hot springs that was once used by health seekers in the late 1800s, but all the buildings have collapsed from the weight of a century of high-country snow. An old ghost town can also be found on the property; and if you look hard enough, you'll find a historic corral that was built by the Indians to trap wild mustangs. In the years that followed, Kit Carson and his men fought a battle at this site.

The spirit of the West is truly alive at the Don K Ranch. Here you can relax by the pool with a tall fanciful drink, take a nature walk (eagles, hummingbirds, deer, and mountain lions are just a few of the animals you might see), or you can saddle up and ride into yesteryear. And don't be surprised if Little Joe and Hoss ride up behind you.

Shaw's Warm Spring

Rio Grande County

Location: Private property
Elevation: 8,000 feet
Temperature: 86°F (30°C)
Flow: 34 to 52 gallons per minute

The original resort at Shaw's Warm Spring (six miles north of Del Norte) is only a memory, and the spring-fed pool that is twenty-five feet from the spring is now empty. Today a small cluster of houses has been built on this site, one of which has tapped the old spring to fill a private indoor swimming pool.

Although Shaw's Warm Spring offers nothing for the tourist today, you still might pass through the town of Del Norte on your way to Rainbow Hot Springs and Pagosa Springs. This is a good place to stock up on film and buy all those odds and ends you might need for the trip into Fun Valley and Rio Grande National Forest. If you're looking for a place to take a driving break, the Speedy Burger Restaurant has good coffee and the best homemade cinnamon rolls in town.

Del Norte is also a good place to fill up your water jugs. In the center of town is an ancient artesian well that is still used by the townspeople, and the thirsty traveler is invited to stop and drink his fill. During the 1800s this well was located in the middle of the crossroads of Grand and Columbia avenues. In 1933 new stones for the well were shaped by state-penitentiary prisoners and shipped to Del Norte. Then the well was moved to its present site on the corner. A word of caution: The high mineral content of the water could damage your car if it is used in the radiator.

Steamboat Springs

Routt County

Location: 150 springs scattered throughout the Yampa Valley
Elevation: 6,695 feet

The whole town of Steamboat Springs is one large playground of hot springs and is one of the brightest resort towns in the state of Colorado. Here you can enjoy a romp around many forgotten fountains.

Thirty years ago Steamboat was considered the "cowiest of cow towns"; now it's known far and wide as "ski town U.S.A.," and it's no wonder, for here you'll encounter some of the finest Nordic and alpine skiing conditions in the country.

There are over 150 springs in the Steamboat area; only a fraction of them are used for recreation, and most of them have been neglected and were forgotten years ago.

The Utes originally called this valley of springs the Yampa (Big Medicine). When the first pioneers moved into the area, which resulted in the bloody Meeker Massacre, the Utes retreated to reservations, leaving the rich Yampa Valley behind. The new settlers gave the area another name: The rhythmic chugging of a large spring's blowhole, which could be heard for a couple of miles, brought to mind the steamboats used on the great Mississippi River in the 1800s. From then on the new settlement was called Steamboat Springs.

Spring Tour

1. On the northwest end of town (south of U.S. 40) is a small park with a few picnic tables. Here, across from the library, you'll find Soda

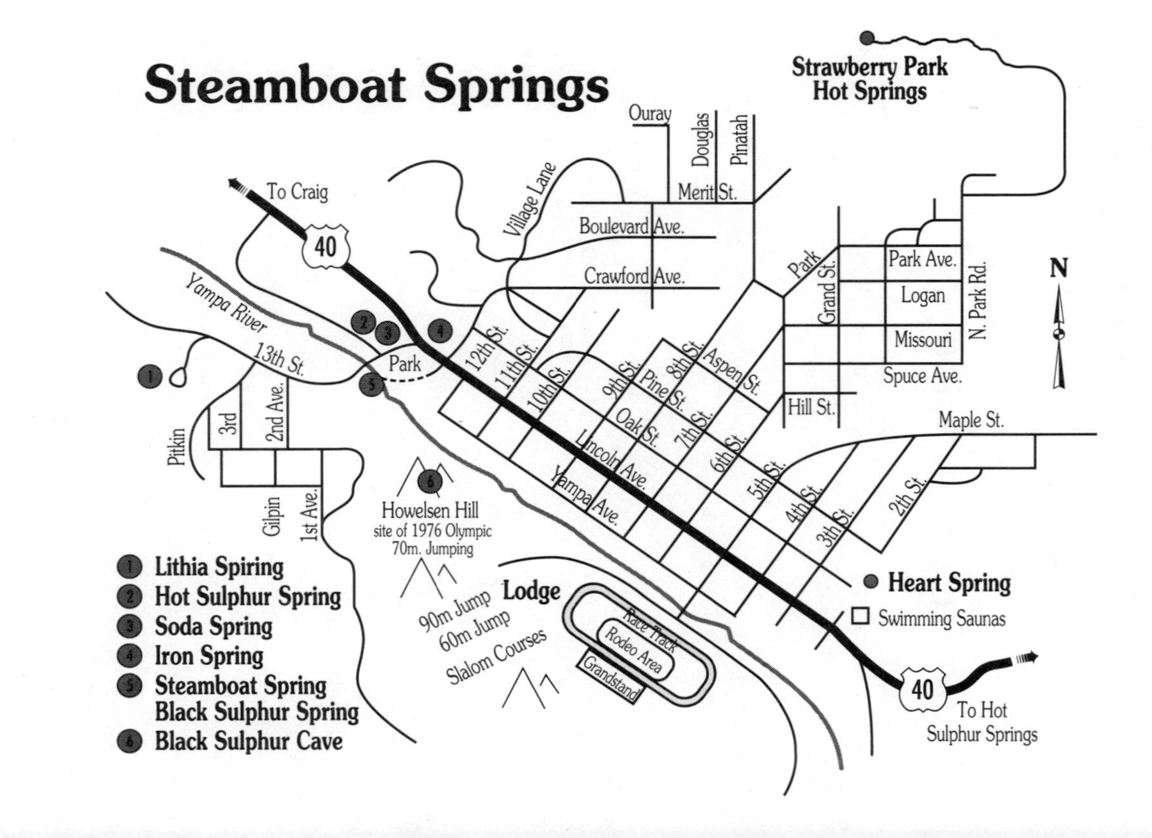
Steamboat Springs
Strawberry Park
Hot Springs
Ouray
Douglas
Pinatah
Merit St.
To Craig
40
Village Lane
Boulevard Ave.
Crawford Ave.
Park
Grand St.
Park Ave.
Logan
Missouri
N. Park Rd.
N
Spuce Ave.
Hill St.
Yampa River
13th St.
Park
12th St.
11th St.
10th St.
9th St.
8th St.
Aspen St.
Pine St.
Oak St.
7th St.
6th St.
5th St.
4th St.
3th St.
2th St.
Maple St.
Lincoln Ave.
Yampa Ave.
Pitkin
3rd
2nd Ave.
Gilpin
1st Ave.
Howelsen Hill
site of 1976 Olympic
70m. Jumping
90m Jump
60m Jump
Slalom Courses
Lodge
Race Track
Rodeo Area
Grandstand
Heart Spring
Swimming Saunas
40
To Hot
Sulphur Springs
1 Lithia Spiring
2 Hot Sulphur Spring
3 Soda Spring
4 Iron Spring
5 Steamboat Spring
Black Sulphur Spring
6 Black Sulphur Cave

Spring and Hot Sulphur Spring. Around the turn of the century, cattlemen built a cement horse trough over Sulphur Spring, and they used to herd their cattle and horses there to drink the mineral water. One old-time rancher told me that he took his horses there once, but he could never get any of them to drink the water. Well, you know the old saying.

2. North of the park on the other side of U.S. 40 you'll find Iron Spring.

3. Steamboat Spring, located with many other springs—Black Sulphur Spring and Narcissus Spring—is across the bridge from the park on the south side of the Yampa River. It has long since ceased to chug, and the water that once spewed fifteen feet in the air has been reduced to a small trickle of mineral water. Many believe that the blasting done by the railroad crippled the spring many years ago, but I stumbled across an obscure historical pamphlet (*Indian Echoes,* by Dr. John A. Campbell), which led me to believe that there just might be another story of the destruction of the great Steamboat Spring.

This pamphlet had an introduction written by Marcellus Merrill and included a few of his early childhood memories. He tells a story of how he and his friends, Maury and Buster, used to drop rocks in the spring to see how high they would go. From the dates and a few clues mentioned in the article, I figured that Mr. Merrill was now living in Denver. I found his name in the phone book and decided to give him a call to find out if he was the boy who put too large a rock in the famous spring and so stopped it from sounding like a steamboat whistle and spouting like a geyser. I put the question to him bluntly, and he countered with a good-natured laugh: "Well, we all dropped a few rocks down the spring, but when it stopped spouting water, Maury told me I had to go over there to get that big rock out of the hole. I was only nine years old at the time. This was back in 1909, the same year the railroad came through. Maybe the railroad stopped the spring from gushing, or maybe I had something to do with it; I don't know which; noboby knows for sure."

4. Across the road from Steamboat Spring you'll see the old railroad depot (now the Fine Arts Center), which was built by the townspeople in 1908. Arts and crafts for sale are on display.

5. As Twenty Mile Road (Thirteenth Street) curves to the west, you'll pass Second and Third avenues. The next gravel road on your left will take you to Lithia Spring.

6. On your way back, head up to Howelsen Hill (named after a Norwegian who introduced a European style of skiing here in 1914). This was one of the few sites to be considered for the 1976 Olympic ski jumping event, and it offers the best scenic view in town. Black Sulphur Cave is also located here. The Ute Indians once used the cave as a form of torture by imprisoning their enemies inside the dark recesses of the earth. The asphyxiating sulphurous gases had a deadly effect.

7. Note: Most of the springs are located near the Yampa River, which is a good river for angling. Unfortunately, it seems that the whitefish outnumber the trout. North of town you'll find two excellent fishing spots, Hahns Peak Lake and Steamboat Lake. The have-gun-will-travel set will find superb hunting around Steamboat.

8. Hot Springs—just north of town on a good gravel road—is a natural hot spring with water hot enough to boil your eggs for lunch. It's a great place to picnic and camp. (See Strawberry Park, page 138.)

9. Heart Spring is a historic heart-shaped pool located behind the recreation center. (See Steamboat Health and Recreation Association, page 135.)

Steamboat Springs

Routt County

Steamboat Springs Health and Recreation Association
Box 1211
136 Lincoln Avenue
Steamboat Springs, Colorado 80477
(303) 879-1828

Location: At the southeast edge of town, just off U.S. 40
Elevation: 6,695 feet
Temperature: 102°F (39°C)
Flow: 140 gallons per minute
Services: Hot mineral pools and saunas, tubular water slide, two low boards and one high board for diving, tennis courts, and snack bar. Suits, towels, and deck chairs are available as rentals.

(See map on page 132.)

Steamboat Springs as a place to live it up is a familiar story to the Colorado traveler; less well known is the Steamboat Health and Recreation Center—for those who have had everything and want to recover from it.

The spring ski season grinds to a halt sometime during mid-April, culminating in the Steamboat Springs Stampede (a three-week spring festival), but the recreation center is open year-round to serve townspeople as well as tourists.

Its present eminence dates back to the early nineteenth century, when Indians prowled this land. This was a favorite hunting and camping ground of the Utes, who often wintered along the lower Yampa River and

The historic Heart Spring. *(Courtesy Colorado Geological Survey)*

fought desperately to keep other tribes from invading their sacred valley. As a matter of fact, the Battle of Steamboat Springs was fought near the present site of the Heart Spring. Yarmony, a Ute chief who died around the turn of the century, told the story of this famous battle. Back in the early 1800s, when Yarmony was eight years old, a band of Arapahos took the Utes by surprise. In the dead of the night, when the moon was round and yellow, the Arapahos traveled from North Park over Buffalo Pass and along the Arapaho Trail until they reached the valley. Bloody warfare followed. Yarmony's father was cut down by an arrow and buried near the present site of the bathhouse. From that day on, it is said that Chief Yarmony visited these springs annually.[1]

The first white settlers (the James H. Crawford family) to use the springs arrived in 1874 via Gore Pass. As the story goes, James Crawford was out tracking game when he stumbled upon the springs. He rushed home, grabbed a shovel, loaded his family on a buckboard wagon, and returned to the springs. By digging holes around the springs, the Crawfords enjoyed the luxury of a hot Indian-style bath.

Ever since 1887, when the first frame bathhouse was built, people have enjoyed these springs. In 1909 a stone building was constructed near Heart Spring (a historic, heart-shaped pool), but it wasn't until 1969 that the present facility was built. Today it is one of the cleanest and most modern municipal recreation centers in the state, and new improvements are being made every day. Here you are about five minutes from the ski slopes. Travel a few blocks northwest of the bathhouse and you'll find yourself in the center of Steamboat action: shops, motels, restaurants, and bars with good beer.

Notes

1. John A. Campbell, *Indian Echoes: Tales of Early Western Colorado* (Denver: Marcellus Merrill, 1970), p. 3.

Strawberry Park Hot Springs

Routt County

Strawberry Park Hot Springs
P.O. Box 773332
Steamboat Springs, Colorado 84047
(303) 879-0342

Location: Eight miles north of Steamboat Springs. Take Seventh Street to Park Road; turn north and drive seven miles to Hot Springs Creek.
Elevation: 7,000 feet
Temperature: Springs ranging from 124° to 147°F (51° to 64°C)
Flow: Springs ranging from 2 to 50 gallons per minute
Services: Six rustic cabins, bathhouse with showers, wood-burning sauna. Open 10 A.M. to midnight all year. Admission fee. Visa and MasterCard accepted.

(See map on page 132.)

There are very few hot springs in the state of Colorado that are as much fun in the winter as they are in the summer, but Strawberry Park Hot Springs provides the best of both worlds. The steep gravel road that leads to the springs takes you through a wide glaciated valley. In the summer you can drive right up to the springs, but in the winter you usually have to park about two miles away and ski the rest of the distance. This is not a trail for superathletes only; a novice to the sport could easily handle it.

Although the primitive hot springs are the main attraction for the kick-and-glide set, many come here to relax, unwind, and get away from it all.

Here, surrounded by rolling mountains, meadows, and the Routt National Forest, you can ski into a winter wonderland. This is one of the most unique winter experiences imaginable.

If you approach Strawberry Park at twilight, the steam from the springs rises into the smoky light. The effect is one of devastation: it looks like the aftermath of some hideous firebombing. But once you enter the smoking rubble and disappear beind a curtain of warm steam, you'll feel as if you've died and gone to hot-springs heaven. Another world opens up right before your eyes. You'll see six terraced rock pools. Hot mineral water from a group of hot springs runs down the side of the mountain and mixes with the cold creek water. The result: a perfect 100°F bath.

I once heard a young man say that the next time he visited the springs he was going to bring a couple of lobsters to cook in the hot water. This might be a little extravagant, but wine chilled in snow and cheese from a rucksack sounds kind of nice. You could even top it off with a couple of boiled eggs. It's always warm and green by the springs, even when there are snowdrifts everywhere else; that's what makes it so enjoyable. After you're done soaking, you might want to ski out toward Mad Creek to the elk-grazing area for a few photographs.

Known as Routt Hot Springs to the Colorado Geological Survey, these springs are known locally as Strawberry Park Hot Springs, and they have had one of the most conspicuous recreational uses in the state of Colorado. For years, people had been skinny-dipping at the springs, which caused a dilemma for the town of Steamboat Springs. In 1979, dozens of bathers were arrested and found guilty of indecent exposure, but the raids didn't discourage the skinny-dippers. As soon as "No Nude Bathing" signs were posted, they were promptly torn down and used as firewood.

Today the hot springs are managed by Don Johnson (not the movie star), who lives in an old Victorian house down the road from this wilderness oasis. He has been developing the property for the past ten years, and he's making more improvements every day. Although the hot mineral water is now channeled into a series of rock-and-masonry pools situated along the riverbank, the hot springs still retain a feeling of primitive naturalness while providing a full range of soaking temperatures. Bathing suits are required during the day except on specialty days, but after dark, swimwear is optional.

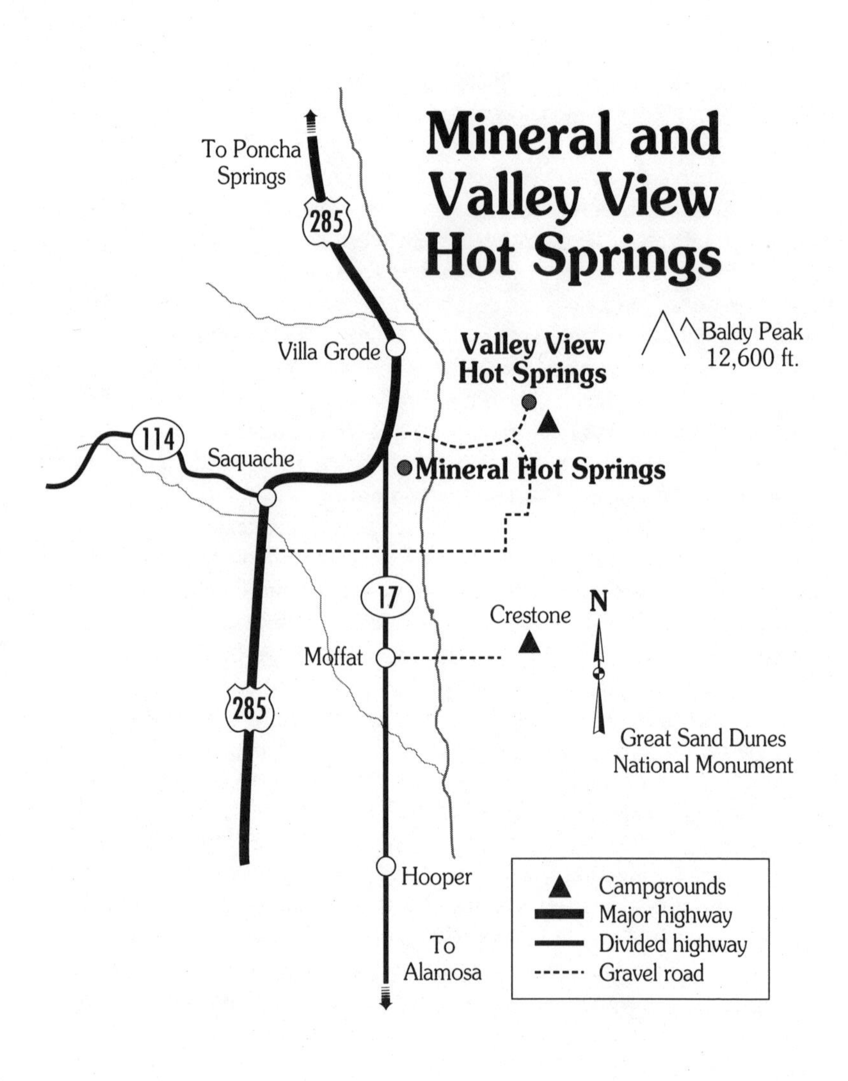
Mineral and
Valley View
Hot Springs
To Poncha
Springs
285
Villa Grode
Valley View
Hot Springs
Baldy Peak
12,600 ft.
114
Saquache
Mineral Hot Springs
17
Crestone
N
Moffat
285
Great Sand Dunes
National Monument
Hooper
To
Alamosa
Campgrounds
Major highway
Divided highway
Gravel road

Mineral Hot Springs

Saguache County

Location: Northern part of the San Luis Valley at the junction of U.S. 285 and Route 17
Elevation: 7,740 feet
Temperature: 124° to 140°F (51° to 60°C)
Flow: 200 gallons per minute
Services: Status uncertain; inquire locally.

This is the site of the old Chamberlain Hot Springs. Although the resort was neglected and unattended for many years, it was possible to take a hot tub here until about 1979. The facility has since been closed to the public. Most of the buildings are empty and decaying, and the pools and sweat baths are filled with rotting wood and broken glass. This property is now part of the North Chamberlain Swine Unit, a hog farm dedicated to keeping bacon on our tables.

Two groups of springs emerge from about thirty separate sources. The water comes from stream alluvium in the San Luis Valley. Many tertiary lava flows have been discovered in the Sangre de Cristo Mountains to the west. The source that heats these waters is probably the same source that supplied the lava flows. The water is used to heat the Spring Motel, a small stucco building that is used to house hog-farm workers.

There is nothing here for the tourist, unless you like to look at lonely old buildings and remember the way things once were, but rumor has it that the property has been sold and that there are plans to clean up the old place and open it to the public. Perhaps this is one hot spring that will be saved and preserved for future generations.

Sand Dunes Swimming Pool Well

Saguache County

Location: Private property
Elevation: 8,000 feet
Temperature: 111°F (44°C)
Flow: None

If you drive into Hooper after 8:00 P.M., the only thing that you'll find open is Don's Place, a funky little roadhouse that serves beer and packaged burritos. The pace is slow, the music is country, and if you shoot pool you'll get along with old Don just fine. Don knows just about everything that happens in town, and he can point you in the direction of the springs. He'll tell you that you can still go up and look at the old place, but you can't go swimming. Be prepared for a rather bland experience.

Situated along the western base of the Sangre de Cristo Range west of that ever-changing sea of sand called the Great Sand Dunes National Monument, is the Sand Dunes Hot Springs. This was once a large community swimming pool, and just a few years ago it was used as a fish farm for growing catfish. Today the catfish tanks are empty. The new owners use the thermal water to heat their home, and although they have refilled the old pool and entertain thoughts of raising alligators, they have no intention of opening it to the public.

Valley View Hot Springs

Saguache County

Valley View Hot Springs
Box 175
Villa Grove, Colorado 81155

Location: Ten miles south of Villa Grove at the junction of U.S. 285 and Route 17, take gravel road due east eight miles; keep to your left when the road forks.
Elevation: 8,700 feet
Temperature: 90° to 97°F (32° to 36°C)
Flow: 300 gallons per minute
Services: Six cabins, tent spaces, free firewood, restrooms, and showers. No credit cards. No reservations. No food services. Open all year. Membership.

(See map on page 140.)

Located in the Sangre de Cristo Mountains, Valley View Hot Springs more than lives up to its name: It promises an experience that is both unusual and satisfying. This beautifully secluded shanty spa has a large swimming pool, a large natural-bottom pool for communal soaking, and five smaller shell-like rock ponds for private soaking, all with dazzling wraparound views of the San Luis Valley. The accommodations here are very rustic; there's no electricity or modern plumbing. Since reservations aren't accepted, the cabins are available on a first-come, first-served basis, so anyone who visits the springs should be prepared to camp out.

During the summer season it is also desirable to carry gear capable of insulating you against those cool mountain nights. Even if you're lucky enough to get a cabin, you'll find that a wood-burning stove provides the only heat. Another thing to remember is that the closest services are ten miles away, in the town of Villa Grove. So stock up on the necessities beforehand, because you won't want to be traveling the bone-rattling dirt road that leads to the springs more than you have to.

Seekers of real solitude will find a tranquil utopia up at Valley View. A cluster of small cabins is perched on a cool wooded mountainside along a babbling creek. There are no telephones, no room service, no pretensions, just a friendly informal place (and by that I mean that people tend to walk around naked here), well suited to couples but not uncomfortable if one goes alone. This is a great place to relax; it is ideal for reading, writing, sleeping, or just watching the spectacular technicolor sunsets.

Valley View is a no-frills resort, requiring the least cash and offering the least flash, yet the lonely pastoral setting can't be matched anywhere in the world. If you're one who takes leisure seriously, you'll find this rustic retreat to be a thoroughly revitalizing experience. The air is pure, the water is pure, and with all that purity around one feels a kind of physical and spiritual purity, too.

The Utes first used the springs before the white man came and homesteaded this land in the 1800s. By the turn of the century, the springs were being developed as a resort; this is when the original concrete pool and cabins were built (the Elm Cabin was once a general store used by miners). Fortunately, at this time interest in hot springs was declining as advances in medicine were gradually pushing health spas out of business. The resort was never completed, and today the delicate landscape remains as beautiful as it was a hundred years ago. Unfortunately, the accommodations haven't changed much since then; however, a hydroelectric system has been built on the creek, and it supplies some of the buildings and cabins with power. The bathroom contains toilets, showers, and sinks.

Although Valley View Hot Springs is well off the beaten path and advertised by word of mouth, so many people have discovered it that the owners have implemented a membership program (memberships are sold once a year starting November 1) to protect against overuse of the property. But if you restrict your visit to weekdays in the early spring or autumn, when the crowds are thin, the owners allow nonmembers to use the springs for a moderate price. Since the sanitation problem is of great concern to everybody who visits the springs, the owners suggest that you leave your dog at home.

If your tastes tend to regal hotels, gourmet dining, or souvenir-filled gift shops, Valley View Hot Springs is not likely to send you into paroxysms of delight. But if you respond to the rugged romance of the outdoors and you just happen to be driving along the High Plains on U.S. 285, looking for an interesting way to pass the time, head up toward the hot springs. It's a unique little oasis totally separated from the outside world, a perfect place to share quiet moments with that special loved one. And, of course, the view isn't bad either.

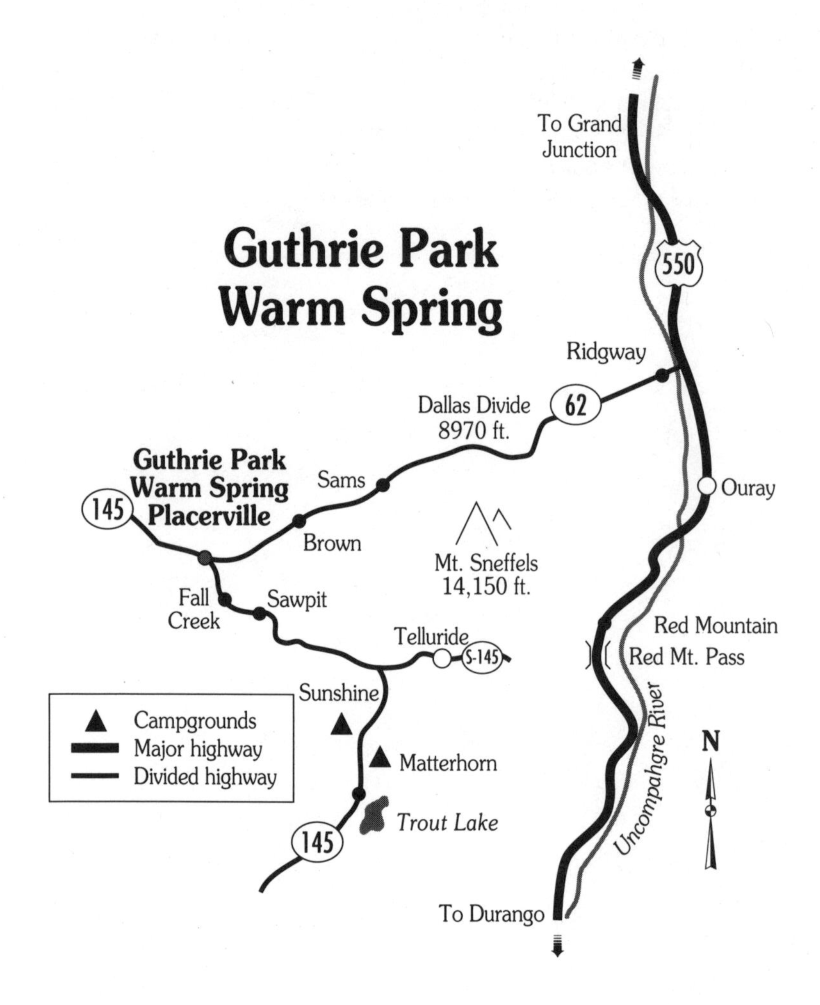
Guthrie Park
Warm Spring
To Grand
Junction
550
Ridgway
62
Dallas Divide
8970 ft.
Guthrie Park
Warm Spring
Placerville
145
Sams
Brown
Ouray
Mt. Sneffels
14,150 ft.
Fall
Creek
Sawpit
Red Mountain
Red Mt. Pass
Telluride
S-145
Sunshine
Campgrounds
Major highway
Divided highway
Matterhorn
Trout Lake
145
Uncompahgre River
N
To Durango

Lemon Hot Spring

San Miguel County

Guthrie Park Warm Spring
Box 26
Placerville, Colorado 81430

Location: Route 145 to the town of Placerville on the west bank of the San Miguel River
Elevation: 7,500 feet
Temperature: 91°F (33°C)
Flow: 8 gallons per minute
Services: No credit cards. Close to the town of Placerville. Open daylight hours all year.

Seventeen miles northwest of Telluride is the tiny town of Placerville. Across from the general store is a dirt road that crosses the river and winds around behind a small group of mobile homes. At the end of the road there is a brown ranch-style home perched on the side of a hill; underneath it is the deepest thermal cave in the state. This is not really a resort; it's a small soaking pool that can only accommodate two or three people at a time. It is located at the end of an old mining tunnel.

Although the tunnel is wired with electricity, the owner wore a hard hat (complete with carbide lamp) when he gave me a tour. "Slamming your head on the low rocky ceiling is no fun," he explained.

As we walked, I noticed a few mazelike passages leading in various directions, and even though they were sealed off with heavy-duty plastic, an occasional blast of cool air swept through the main tunnel. The sound of trickling water echoed in the dim, dark grotto.

According to the owner, the water that fed the small pool was ancient water, which means that it's not resupplied from above. He also said that the water has cooled off in the last few years.

Placerville is hardly the most exciting hot spring in Colorado, and it's definitely not for those who like their water really hot. Still, I like it—but then, I usually like down-home places and friendly folks.

Minerals and Nutrition*

Calcium . . . . Calcium is needed for bones, teeth, cartilage, proper blood clotting, nerve and muscle functioning.

Copper . . . . Copper is an essential element for supporting life. In small amounts it is needed to form hemoglobin.

Fluoride . . . . Fluoride has never been proven to be essential to life, but it is an important constituent of the elastic fibers of the skin and the surfaces of bones and teeth. It gives hardness and stability.

Iron . . . . Iron is essential in human nutrition, since it combines with protein to make hemoglobin, the coloring matter of red blood cells. It also aids in the distribution of oxygen throughout the body.

Magnesium . . . . Magnesium is needed for the production and transfer of energy, muscle maintenance, protein synthesis, and many chemical reactions in the body.

Manganese . . . . Manganese is necessary for bone development, reproduction, nerves, and the buildup and breakdown of protein cycles in the body.

Phosphorous . . . . Phosphorous, stored in the bones, is closely associated with calcium and vitamin D. Produces energy and builds new tissue.

Potassium . . . . Potassium is needed for proper muscle function, iron balance, and cell nutrition.

Selenium . . . . Selenium has been shown to reduce all types of cancer, helps prevent chromosome breakage. Studies have shown that in communities where selenium intake is low, the cancer rate is high.

Silica . . . . Silica gives strength to bones, nerves, mucous membranes, hair, and nails.

Sodium . . . . A sodium fluid bathes every cell in the body.

Sulphur . . . . Sulphur is found in every cell of the body, but the cells that contain the most are skin, hair, and nails, and the fluids in joints and vertebral discs.

Zinc . . . . Zinc is involved in tissue nutrition and protein-building. It is also needed in tissue repair.

*From *Zinc and Other Micro-Nutrients,* by Dr. Carl C. Pfeiffer (New Canaan, Conn.: Keats Publishing, Inc., 1978).

Index of Springs

Selected Reading

Andrist, Ralph K. *The Long Death: The Last Days of the Plains Indians.* New York: Macmillan Publishing Co., Inc., 1964.

Bancroft, Caroline. *Glenwood's Early Glamor.* Boulder, Colo.: Johnson Publishing, 1958.

Barrett, James K., and Richard Howard Pearl. *An Appraisal of Colorado's Geothermal Resources.* Bulletin 39. Denver: Colorado Geological Survey Department of Natural Resources, 1978.

Brown, Constance. "But It's Always Hot-Spring Time in the Rockies." *Smithsonian* (Nov. 1977), pp. 90-97.

Campbell, John A. *Indian Echoes: Tales of Early Western Colorado.* Denver: Marcellus Merrill, 1970.

Colorado Cities and Places. Chicago: Chicago, Rock Island & Pacific Railway, 1890.

Daniels, Helen Sloan. *The Ute Indians of Southwestern Colorado.* Durango, Colo.: Durango Public Library, 1941.

Fitch, William Edward. *Mineral Waters of the U.S. and American Spas.* Philadelphia: Lea and Feibiger, 1927.

George, R. D., et al. *Mineral Waters of Colorado.* Colorado Geological Survey Bulletin 11. Denver: Eames Bros., State Printers, 1920.

Gilland, Mary Ellen. *Summit: A Gold Rush History of Summit County.* Silverthorn, Colo.: Alpenrose Press, 1980.

Howbert, Irving. *The Indians of the Pike's Peak Region.* New York: The Knickerbocker Press, 1914.

James, Billy Mac. *Health-Seekers in the Southwest, 1817-1900.* Norman, Okla.: University of Oklahoma Press, 1967.

Loam, Jayson. *Hot Springs and Pools of the Northwest.* Santa Barbara: Capra Press, 1980.

Meeker, Josephine. *The Ute Massacre!: Brave Miss Meeker's Captivity!* Cheyenne, Wyo.: Vic Press-Books, 1975.

Morgan, Dale L. *Jedediah Smith and the Opening of the West.* Lincoln/London: Bison Books, University of Nebraska Press, 1953.

Parris, Lloyd E. *Caves of Colorado.* Boulder, Colo.: Pruett Publishing Company, 1973.

Pearl, Richard Howard. *Geothermal Resources of Colorado.* Special Pub. 2. Denver: Colorado Geological Survey Department of Natural Resources, 1972.

Pearl, Richard M. *Springs of Colorado.* Colorado Springs: Earth Science Publishing Company, 1975.

Rockwell, Wilson. *The Utes—A Forgotten People.* Denver: Allan Swallow, Sage Books, 1956.

Smith, Don. *Chalk Creek to the Past.* Privately printed, 1958.

Smith, Duane A. *Rocky Mountain Mining Camps: The Urban Frontier.* Lincoln/London: Bison Books, University of Nebraska Press, 1974.

Swift, Kim. *Heart of the Rockies: A History of the Salida Area.* Colorado Springs: Century One Press, 1980.

Talmadge, Marian, and Iris Gilmore. *Colorado Hi-ways and Bi-ways: A Comprehensive Guide to Picturesque Trails and Tours.* 4 vols. Denver: Heather Enterprises, Inc., 1967.

Vandenbusche, Duane, and Duane A. Smith. *A Land Alone: Colorado's Western Slope.* Boulder, Colo.: Pruett Publishing Company, 1981.